CHINESE ADVENTURE

A RIDE ALONG THE GREAT WALL

by

Robin Hanbury-Tenison O.B.E., F.R.G.S.

Copyright © Robin Hanbury-Tenison

First published in 1987

ISBN: 1-59048-122-4

The Long Riders' Guild Press 2004

Foreword

By Catherine Waridel

For centuries men have been travelling across continents, and ever since man domesticated horses, camels and others, there have been "Long Riders." Traders, ambassadors, armies, adventurers and missionaries rode from western countries to China, and *vice versa*. Few of these left written evidence of their journeys. From the Middle Ages we have rich texts, such as those of Marco Polo, Plano Carpini and William of Rubruck. The Mongol Empire had reopened the roads between East and West, roads which were closed again under Tamerlane.

The twentieth century saw many explorers, scholars, and a few Long Riders who gave us tales of their journeys.

One in particular must be mentioned: Ella Maillart. She wrote a book, *Oasis interdites (Forbidden Journey)*, about her journey with Peter Fleming in 1935 from Beijing to Kashgar, then across the mountains of Pamir to Kashmir. "A book of happiness" is how Nicholas Bouvier described it. Ella Maillart had given him a copy of the book with this dedication: "Un voyage où il ne se passe rien, mais ce rien me comblera toute ma vie." ("A journey where nothing happened, but this nothing will satisfy me for the rest of my life.")

In 1985 I read a new French translation of the incomparable Friar William Rubruck's account of his journey to Mongolia in the thirteenth century. It was as if he had put his arm around my shoulder and said, "follow me." I did follow him, for almost four years, when I rode alone along his exact itinerary, from the Crimea to Mongolia, through Ukraine, Russia, Kazakhstan and Xinjiang. In spite of many difficulties – the climate, hunger, thirst, exhaustion, long days in the saddle, short nights –nothing could interfere with my pleasure in following William's trail. The journey was magic – I felt free to fill my soul with infinite space and eternal time, to nourish my heart with contentment and serenity. I achieved my aim: to compare the people, culture and traditions of the twentieth century with those of the thirteenth century. Rubruck's sponsor was Saint Louis, King of France. I had money I had saved.

Recently I read *Chinese Adventure – A Ride along The Great Wall* by Robin Hanbury-Tenison. Robin and his wife Louella rode on horseback for a thousand miles along this great monument. Because of the small-minded Chinese bureaucrats, they were not able to repeat the journey made by W. E. Geil in 1908 along the whole length of the wall.

The Great Wall – what a dream to see its history! It runs for about 2,000 miles, like a snake curving itself into the shape of the landscape. It was born more than two thousand years ago, and over many centuries it cost the lives of millions of workers, soldiers and peasants who were deported and forced to work in tough and inhumane conditions.

In the third century Tch'en Li wrote the following verses in his *Ballad of the Soldier:*

> *"A man would prefer to die in a battle, armed*
> *For how to stand, in trouble and agony, to build the Wall?*
> *Long, long. The Great Wall is without an end.*
> *Stretched the length of its three thousand stades."*

It is difficult to imagine the volume of suffering which fills each stone in the wall – which can only be compared with the Pyramids of Egypt.

Robin Hanbury-Tenison hopes that the Chinese authorities will soon be in a position to help people to ride the whole length of this fabulous monument. *"I beg them (the travellers) to do it on horses."* I fully agree with him, because riding allows you to look all around you, without bothering too much about the road. Also, even after innumerable hours in the saddle, I felt like a centaur. I was full of love and admiration for my horses' strength and endurance, as they loved me in return for my will to succeed. Horses are full of love, if we ask them.

The Chinese authorities are no different from ours. They are usually the first victims of the system. Instead of spreading money around, it is better to start with smiles and courtesy. Make them believe that your project is their idea and that they will bask in the glory of your success. Massage their pride so it overrides their fear of the system. Mental corruption? I succeeded. I obtained everything I needed, and more. "Civility" is a language understood all over the world.

If a Long Rider wishes to undertake a similar adventure, I beg him or her to take Robin Hanbury-Tenison's book as a bible, as I carried Rubrick's account of his journey. Robin's book will be the key to success, and help you to avoid wasting time and energy.

Catherine Waridel
Geneva, 2003

CONTENTS

For Louella, to whom I give inadequate credit in this book for her toughness, cheerfulness and courage, which were what really got us through.

And for Merlin, who was the best outcome of our French ride . . .

Robin and Louella Hanbury-Tenison's ride along the full 1,000 mile length of the Great Wall of China with three pairs of Chinese horses is well in keeping with the British tradition for eccentricity. In that respect it could not have been a more appropriate choice. The Great Wall must rank as a grand piece of eccentricity itself. It may be one of the wonders of the world today, but as a means of keeping out invaders it did not prove to be entirely effective.

Nonetheless the journey was a magnificent adventure and a remarkable achievement, and it has given rise to this enthralling book.

For those who have already visited China, and also for those who may feel like taking advantage of China's revived hospitality for foreign visitors, this account of an epic journey provides a view of northern China which few tourists are ever likely to be able to see for themselves.

ACKNOWLEDGEMENTS

The list of those who helped us is endless and should include innumerable Chinese people along our route who showed us kindness and whose names we often never knew. Many others are referred to in the text. Special mention should, however, be made of Sir Richard and Lady Evans, John Dennis and all the staff of the British Embassy in Peking, who went out of their way to smooth our path; John Swire and lots of nice people at Cathay Pacific; David Davies and Owen Price for generous provisions from Dairy Farms; Victor Chu for being our prop and stay in Hong Kong; the Marconi Company; Eric Chan of the Jianguo Hotel, Peking; Jane Talbot-Smith of Cornwall for repairs and modifications to our saddles; Dr David Giles of Bude and Dr Eric Goon of Peking for medical supplies and advice; Paul Woodman, of the Permanent Committee for Geographical Names, for help with obscure place names along the Wall; Patrick Lui, the film maker, for priceless advice and Ning Chang for waving her magic wand.

Hou Xiangjing, Hu Ke and above all Li Zhaofeng of CIEC who toiled ceaselessly on our behalf, while those above them, Jing Shuping and Gu Xiancheng, gave weighty support to our plans. But it is to Rong Yiren, president of both CIEC and CITIC, our co-sponsor with His Royal Highness Prince Philip, President of the World Wildlife Fund, that our most humble thanks must go.

Finally there is no shadow of a doubt that without Robbie Lyle's help and enthusiasm none of what follows would have happened.

NOTE

With the exceptions of Peking (Beijing), Canton (Guangzhou), Hong Kong (Xianggang), Tibet (Xizang) and the river Yangze (Changjiang), the familiar English names which the Chinese themselves do not find offensive, I have attempted to use the new Chinese Pinyin spelling throughout.

During our time in China £1 was worth about 5 yuan and US $1 about 4 yuan.

INTRODUCTION

On completing a long journey, there is one question which springs irresistibly to the lips of almost all a traveller's friends and relations. Images and impressions crowd the traveller's mind; he bursts with stories about his recent experiences, which he would be happy to share; but at first the world seems to shy away from hearing these.

'Where are you off to next?' they ask. It is in the need to answer this question positively that most journeys are conceived.

So it was with China.

In 1984 Louella and I bought two white Camargue horses on the Mediterranean coast and rode them back across France to our stock farm in Cornwall.* This ride, which was originally undertaken simply as a romantic and pleasant way of bringing the horses home, seemed to touch a chord with all sorts of people. The reflex question was asked with a peculiar intensity and demanded an answer.

My previous journeys had been quite different. For twenty-five years I had been making ambitious and arduous expeditions to tropical rain forests and across deserts. These too had, if I am honest, been prompted more by a desire to satisfy the 'Where next?' question rather than from an innate wanderlust, but I had been able to persuade myself that they were not entirely selfish and might serve some useful purpose. The books I wrote dealt with serious issues, which I believed affected mankind's welfare and indeed our very survival. The destruction of the rain forests and of the people who live there; the misuse of our planet by thoughtless progress, and the beauty and stability still to be found in the world's remotest corners were my themes. It amused me that when for once we did something unashamedly frivolous and self-indulgent we should find ourselves recognized in supermarkets and besieged with fan letters from an admiring public.

The BBC made a film for television about our ride, covering the start, finish and a few days in the middle. At the very end, after the credits and when we assumed most viewers would have switched off,

*White Horses Over France, published by Granada, 1985

we slipped in a private joke. As the camera pulls away from the two of us on our horses on a Cornish hilltop, Louella turns to me and asks 'Where shall we go next?' I reply, 'How about along the Great Wall of China?' and she answers, 'Now, that really would be something!' So, instead of asking 'Where next?' our friends asked us when we were off to China or, even more maddeningly, whether we had already done it. It seemed we would have to go.

The first thing we found out was that it was impossible. While the door to China is opening wider than it ever has before, there are still large parts of the country that are closed to foreigners and these include most of the regions through which the Great Wall runs. There are really still only two forms of travel which are permitted in China today. One, which is encouraged, is the organized guided tour. Group travel is fairly expensive, but there is now a wide choice of places to visit and a plethora of guide books describing them. Travellers are cared for and organized from the moment they arrive in China until they leave. There will be some hassles because there always are in China and so they will come back with some tall stories and experiences to relate which have given them a glimpse into Chinese life and the Chinese mind. But primarily they will have been able to see and do things advertised in the travel brochure and so they will feel they have had their money's worth. The other is individual travel and this is becoming increasingly popular with specialist travel agencies being set up to advise on the subject and arrange visas. As an up-market individual traveller you see and do many of the same things as the group tourist, often also as part of a group. However, you are able to escape, choose your own itinerary, travel alone by train or plane and sometimes even find a restaurant other than a hotel dining room to visit. You can hire a bicycle to do some independent exploring. But it is the down-market travellers, the student backpackers, who have far the most interesting time in China today.

Their numbers are accelerating and in the cities and regions of China now open to foreigners they are in theory allowed to travel everywhere freely. Every conceivable obstacle is put in their way, but for the enterprising young this simply adds to the fun. It can also be incredibly cheap. Whereas it is accepted official and unashamed policy to charge foreigners at least twice as much as Chinese, students who learn the dodges can find all sorts of ways round the system. Two girls, whose journal I read, spent a month travelling very widely around China for a total cost of £50 each for all their transport, food and accommodation – as much, they pointed out, as the average group tourist pays for a day. They had had a wonderful time, meeting lots of Chinese people, being invited to talk to school classes, staying with the teachers and hitching lifts on lorries, but they were also very aware that they had been pushing their luck a lot of the time. They were

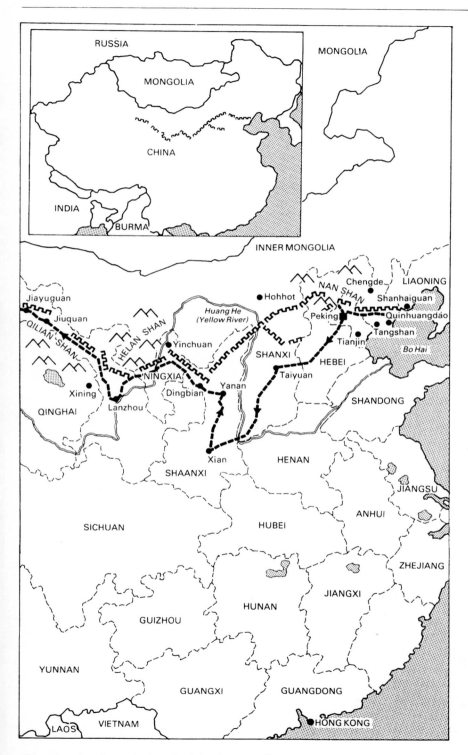

China showing the entire length of the Great Wall.

Contrasting views of the Wall: (*right*) the popular image of the Wall is that of the early fifteenth-century Ming Wall, seen here near Qinglong Qiao (*Anthony J. Lambert*); (*below*) the decayed mud wall of the western end as it skirts the Gobi Desert.

The Aliens' Travel Permit issued to Robin and Louella Hanbury-Tenison.

constantly straying into areas where they should not have been and running the risk of falling foul of the authorities.

Some determined travellers have recently gone further than this and penetrated quite remote parts of China through various subterfuges. One of the more remarkable was Christina Dodwell, who packed a small inflatable canoe in her rucksack so that when passing an interesting stretch of river in a local bus she was able to stop and disappear downstream for days at a time.

Much as we would have liked to have done so, we simply could not just go to China and travel along our proposed route on horses. We would have been arrested at once and deported. We would have to do it legally and officially; very special permission indeed was going to be needed.

We went to see Robbie Lyle, a childhood friend of Louella's, who worked in the City and whose sphere of interest was China. We were advised that he knew how to get things done there better than most, and, unlike everyone else, when we told him of our plans he greeted them with enthusiasm. I have since learnt that Robbie is an incurable optimist, the most valuable trait for anyone wrestling with Chinese bureaucracy. Several times over the next year of planning and negotiation, when I was cast down by what sounded like a final rejection of our proposals or a flat refusal of some specific idea, I would ring him up in despair to tell him the bad news. His reaction was always the same, and it was immensely cheering. 'Ah good!' he would say. 'If they are that positive about it then they are about to give in.' And to our amazement he was nearly always right. We began to rely on him more and more as our guardian angel and it is certain that without his help we would not only never have received permission to go, but we would have given up trying to get it.

There are always excellent reasons for not doing things. A decision to try and make a long independent journey through closed regions of China was going to open a Pandora's Box of problems. There was no precedent for it or anything like it in the last fifty years. We began to hear horrifying stories of the new Chinese habit of fleecing expeditions of vast sums of money. Mountaineers invited to pioneer new routes alongside Chinese climbers found themselves being made to pay inflated prices for transport and supplies for their companions as well as themselves. As a result they needed massive sponsorship. For a time we considered this ourselves. If we were to take our own Camargue horses and ride them along the Wall it would make a rather romantic story that might attract a sponsor. But in the end this idea came to nothing, and in fact it was rather a relief as we had begun to worry about what we would be letting Thibert and Tiki, the French horses, in for. They might catch all sorts of nasty diseases and, if one went lame or fell ill, we would not want to exchange him for another en route.

There were also a great many things happening in our lives which made the idea of being away for three months seem at times far fetched and unnecessary. We did not want to leave our children, who now included a baby boy, born nine months after our French ride. A famous remark made by Dr Johnson in 1788 comforted us when we felt guilty about this. I came across a reference to it while reading about the Great Wall in Luo Zewen's book:

Dr Johnson had become specially interested in China. He was a friend of Lord Macartney, the first ambassador to be sent from Britain to the Chinese court. Johnson would dearly have loved to visit China to see for himself the Great Wall, which he regarded as a wonder of the world. But the opportunity never came.

His companion and biographer, James Boswell, talked to him about this one day, commenting that he, Boswell, would himself like to go and see the Wall of China if he did not have a duty to look after his children. This elicited the scornful response from Johnson: 'Sir, by doing so, you would do what would be of importance in raising your children to eminence. There would be a lustre reflected on them from your spirit and curiosity. They would at all times be regarded as the children of a man who had gone to view the Wall of China. I am serious, Sir.'

Innumerable people from all over the world have 'viewed' the Great Wall since that time, almost all at the short restored section near Peking. Only one foreigner claimed to have travelled from one end to the other; the eccentric American dilettante, William Geil, in 1908.

The farm, too, was undergoing a major upheaval. My share-farming partner, Pancho, had great plans for diversifying our beef and sheep enterprise into red deer and Angora goats. I have always, however, been able to convince myself that things run better on the farm when I am not there and this seemed like a good time to keep out of the way.

As I have said, there are always good reasons for not doing things, but life is short and the more you do the more you get done. Besides, we had by now answered too many people's 'Where next?' questions positively and so we were hoist with China. The longer we went on saying we were planning to do it the more impossible it became to pull out without losing that very Chinese thing, face. I learned much later that the word was out among my colleagues in the exploring world that 'This time Robin really has bitten off more than he can chew' and there was a universal belief that we would fail. But the more we read and researched about China the more excited we became at the prospect of going there whatever the difficulties. Furthermore we looked forward to the possibility of another long happy ride together. As we summed it up at the time there were really only three problems to be resolved; the permission, the money and the horses. We began to work on it and in November 1985 Robbie suggested that I should fly out on a recce to present our idea to the authorities while he was in Peking himself.

I went via Hong Kong as an idea was beginning to take shape, which might resolve the second of our problems, that of money. Why not make this a sponsored ride and raise lots of funds for charity? It seems to be the fashion to do this today and since we made no pretence that our proposed ride had any scientific merit, then we should let some good come from it. Hong Kong was a rich place and a lot of people seemed delighted at the prospect of helping us. I just needed to persuade them that we would succeed. Then I had to convince the powers that be in China itself that they should let us go. Finally I had to track down a couple of suitable horses.

It all seemed so easy when put like that.

THE MIDDLE KINGDOM

The Cathay Pacific flight to Hong Kong passes over one of the wildest and least accessible regions left on earth. Where five nations' borders almost meet on the Tropic of Cancer, hill tribes and war lords defy the authority of government, and local conflicts flare up continuously. The landscape is so broken, the forested hillsides so steep and the rivers so fast flowing that there are few roads and travel overland is painfully slow. Nearly thirty years ago, before Burma restricted all foreign travellers to seven day visas, I travelled beyond Mandalay into this wild country. The Captain kindly let me see it again from the flight deck.

Below us I could see the Irrawaddy, unmistakably wide and muddy, which I went down in 1958 in a paddle steamer, locked in a cage for my own security, they said, in case bandits attacked us from the shore. Now I flew over miles and miles of gloriously undisturbed forest; no signs of life, only the greenery of one of the last true tropical wildernesses on earth.

'We are just about to cross the border into China,' said the Captain.

This was my first sight of China and it was an exciting moment. Suddenly the character of the landscape below changed. A whole mountain top had been cleared of vegetation and there were red scars of erosion on its sides. Even from 30,000 feet I could see terracing on some of the slopes, dirt roads snaking along and clusters of tin-roofed houses glinting in the valleys. I felt a shock of recognition that we were over the most populous nation on earth. I had not expected their presence to be so instantly apparent from the air.

The Fundraising Committee of the Hong Kong branch of the World Wildlife Fund met for a delicious lunch on the thirty-sixth floor of the building above their offices. I was invited to address them and talked so much that I missed out on the food. After telling them about my past track record of expeditions and books, I explained that riding for a charity was a new departure for both Louella and me. However, much of my life had been devoted to conservation of one sort or another and I had worked with the WWF on several occasions. They were welcome to anything they could raise through our journey and we did not mind being used in advertisements if necessary. Someone asked if we had any moral objection to being backed by a tobacco company. This stopped me in my tracks for a moment as Louella has never smoked and I, having given up some years ago, now have the passion of the converted. Still, as long as it was clear that the money was for the WWF and not for us, I could see no problem – and I rather fancied myself as the man in the Marlboro advertisements. We agreed to meet and talk again on my return from China.

I packed several other meetings into my one day in Hong Kong. It is a place where a great deal can be achieved in a very short time. One of the vets at the Jockey Club most kindly gave me a lot of useful advice about buying horses.

'Look for straight tendons,' he said. 'Watch out for enlargement of the fetlock joints. Make sure there are no lumps or bumps around the joints and that you can bend them all the way. Trot them hard and test for lameness – if there's any trace of that don't touch them! Don't worry too much about "splints".'

Although I have ridden all my life, I make no pretence of being a 'horsy' person and I have always had a problem remembering which bits of the horse are which. I tried to look intelligent and took lots of notes, but I also wondered how much choice we would have when it came to the point. He told me that most of the horses he had seen on a recent trip, even up on the Mongolian grassland plains, had been for pulling carts. They had been in good condition with very hardened hooves, so that we should be able to go unshod if there were no blacksmiths.

Greatly reassured to have at last met someone who knew what he was talking about and did not regard our plan as wholly mad, I hurried to a meeting with Owen Price, Managing Director of Dairy Farm. This huge company has grown from a herd of eighty milch cows imported into the colony in 1886 and now controls all sorts of retail and manufacturing businesses, including a large chain of supermarkets. I had an introduction to Owen and planned to do my best to persuade him to supply us with rations for our ride. Instead of having a long talk, however, I found that he was in the middle of an extremely busy afternoon.

I prepared to launch into a long explanation about our plans and hopes to justify my request for help from his company. 'You see,' I said, 'we're planning to ride along the Great Wall of China and we hoped you might give us some food.' Such requests always sound most unlikely at the moment of making them. In the first place my smart tropical suit disappears and I feel myself to be in rags with a begging bowl; in the second place, why on earth should he help us?

'Certainly,' said Owen. 'How much do you need?'

David Griffiths ran from Peking to Hong Kong in 1983. He covered the 2,380 miles in 55 days and was the first foreign long distance runner allowed to run in China. I went to see him at his elegant health club in the centre of Hong Kong and learned that he was planning to run along the Great Wall in six months' time. Our approach to the problems ahead and our motives for attempting to overcome them were so different that we found to our relief that there was no sense of rivalry between us. We liked each other and agreed to pool our ideas and information. David was extraordinarily generous with facts on the ground he had already covered in his preparations and the experience he had gained on his previous run. When I left him I was far better briefed on what to ask for in Peking and what to expect in reply.

The next day I boarded the flight to Peking. As I queued in the aisle, waiting for elderly Chinese gentlemen to stow their copious Hong Kong purchases in the overhead lockers, I caught the eye of the man who was sitting in my seat, ahead. The other passengers were sharply divided between those in suits and ties and those in scruffy jeans. I thought idly as I waited that you can tell a lot from someone's clothes. He wore a faded leather jacket over an open check shirt and he looked like a film director. We sorted out the seats and I discovered that he was, indeed, a director.

He was Mickey Grant, from Dallas, and as we talked I learned that he had recently made the film of another run across China. This was called the Great Friendship Run, and had been accomplished by an American called Stan Cottrell, who had followed much the same route as David Griffiths but had started on the Great Wall just north of Peking and finished at Canton just north of Hong Kong. He knew all about David and I told him we had spent much of the previous day discussing our respective ideas. He was planning further films in China and by the end of the flight we'd made plans for him to film our ride as well, using a Chinese crew to cut the otherwise prohibitive costs.

'How odd that we should be sitting next to each other!' Mickey said.

'Worse than that,' I said. 'You were in my seat. It's a perfect case of synchronicity.'

Mickey introduced me to China. A youngish laid-back Texan with a round mobile face, he was a most unlikely Mandarin speaker, but he had studied the language for three years and had a natural ability to communicate. We took a taxi to the Friendship Store where we entered an unreal 1950s world which went straight to our heads. It was a large department store stocked with the produce of China and it was supposed to be used only by foreigners. Only Foreign Exchange Certificates were accepted there and these could, in theory, only be obtained by visitors to the country. The national currency is the renminbi or 'People's Money' but the two-currency system was beginning to break down and there were lots of Chinese people there.

The atmosphere, layout, designs and fashions were all wildly dated and I felt that I had been transported back thirty years in time. At the fur section, for which the store is famous, I was momentarily subdued by the sight of leopard skin jackets among the fox, wolf, mink and ermine coats. Although China is a signatory of the Convention on International Trade in Endangered Species, conservation is still a very new concept there. The children's department was wonderfully colourful, dominated by hundreds of multi-coloured kites in the shapes of real and mythical animals.

'The best bit's downstairs,' said Mickey, who was into acupuncture and herbal medicines. It was an impressive display and I pored over strange instructions for treating even stranger ailments. There were 'dragons' bones', fossils of prehistoric animals, to be ground up; extracts of toads and lizard as well as ginseng of all sorts, sometimes sold as whole, obscenely shaped roots in glass bottles. The instructions, when translated, recommended cures for boils, hot palms, hot temper, biliousness and grinding teeth. There was artemisia root for burning on the patient's skin, another strange Chinese medical practice called moxibustion.

Mickey bought a do-it-yourself battery-operated electric acupuncture kit and I almost bought a superb scale model of a horse in painted rubber, showing the acupuncture points on one side and its insides exposed on the other. Feeling slightly hysterical we sampled various sorts of tiger balm and sniffed at strangely coloured miniature bottles of essences which the giggly sales girls told us were for every imaginable ailment from impotence to backache.

Back at the Great Wall Hotel we had a sandwich in the totally unreal and incongruous lobby. Two rather shabby old men in white tie and tails were making wonderful music on a piano and violin while the glass external lifts delivering tired tourists to their beds shot up seven storeys past the plants and fountains above our heads. We sat up late talking and making ever wilder plans about filming our ride.

Robbie was not due to arrive for another day and so I had a chance to do some sightseeing. I was so unseasoned in Chinese affairs I believed that I would be spending much of the next fortnight reconnoitring our route, following a few brisk meetings to obtain the necessary permissions in the capital. I now know that it is never like that in China.

Happily a great friend, Nigel Sitwell, was also in town and we were able to share a taxi and the pleasures of the day. We walked in vast Tien An Men Square in crisp, sunny weather, past the masses in from the provinces queuing to be photographed in front of the last remaining giant portrait of Chairman Mao. Then we entered the Forbidden City and were confronted by the breathtaking succession of Heavenly Gates. The crowds did not, to my surprise, then or at any time in China oppress me in the way I had expected from experience elsewhere. Instead the sense of space and sky seemed to lift me above them and I was astounded by the silhouettes of decorated roof tiles: dragons, birds, lions and horses in procession along the graceful curves of roofs. It is a magical place and feels strangely undisturbed, though it has been much restored. A visitor is made to feel alone with all the beauty. A few man-made structures are able to do this, to produce such an overwhelmingly satisfying effect that neither the build-up of excessive expectations, nor the crowds of other tourists, nor the factory chimneys and skyscrapers in the background can make one feel disappointed: the Acropolis, the Taj Mahal, St Peter's, and now The Forbidden City, too.

Ann Bridge, in *The Ginger Griffin,* one of her delightful novels about Peking in the 1920s, describes her heroine Amber bluffing her way past the guards at the gate when the City was closed and deserted.

She found herself on a great paved roadway, at least a hundred yards wide, walled in on each side with narrow cloisters, and closed at the further end by another gateway precisely similar to that through which she had come. On her right the greyish green of thujas showed over the yellow tiles of the cloister, and among them the long golden roof of some hidden building, shining in the brilliant light. There was no one about; pale dead grasses stood up in the cracks between the paving-stones; a mouse ran nimbly through the sunshine to some hidden destination. Vast, deserted, desolate – and incredibly beautiful . . .

The supreme wonder of Chinese architecture lies in its use of space. It is not only in the curved pillared roofs, built to imitate the pole-propped tents of their ancestors, that the architects of the Forbidden City betray their nomadic origin. By a strange skill in proportions, by isolating great pavilions in immense stretches of flagged paving, they have succeeded in bringing into their palace courts the endless spaces of the Gobi desert. The eye travels over the lower walls surrounding each mighty enclosure to distant roof-trees, and beyond these to others more distant still, with a sense of beholding mountain ranges hull-down on vast horizons; the gold of the roofs suggests the wonder of dawn and sunset on far-off snows. The world holds nothing to match this, knows nothing on such a scale. Not even Ang-Kor can approach those areas of granite pavement, those miles of scarlet wall.

There is still an endearing feeling of abandonment and some grass grows in the courtyards and on unrestored roofs. Apart from all the great temples, museums and treasure houses, there are also intimate corners where we felt a concubine or eunuch might appear. Among the trees giving freshness and a sense of country there were rockeries with flights of steps and hidden bamboo gardens. It was easy to escape from the regimented hordes obediently reading the instructions and following the signs. We even found a small stall selling tiny red toffee crab apples on sticks. The toffee and the pips were tooth-cracking hard, but there was a refreshing and delicious explosion of apple taste in the middle.

For a week I suffered my first ordeal by Chinese bureaucracy of delays, frustrations and prevarications. Robbie arrived, full of energy and good humour, but with a great many other problems than mine to sort out. I am not used to being unable to fight my own battles and I chafed at having to wait. I was by now aware, however, that China was not a place where bluster, bribery or bending of the rules would work; I would get nowhere without patient guidance through the uncharted waters ahead, plus a lot of influence and luck. Robbie was my guide; blundering in on my own would do no good and so I had to contain myself impatiently. In between exquisite expensive meals with charming influential Chinese friends of his, who added their polite disbelief at mention of our plans to the more crudely expressed doubts of expatriates with which I was already familiar, I tried to take some exercise as a form of therapy. Robbie liked to go jogging early in the morning and I went with him.

The first couple of days had been crisp and sunny but we came out of the hotel on 15 November to freezing grey smog. This is the date when, regardless of the weather, the power plants which provide centralized heating to Peking start up. All at once chimneys everywhere were disgorging great clouds of smoke and the sun vanished. In our tracksuits, with scarves over our faces and our breath white on the frozen air, we were as anonymous as the shapeless padded figures passing on bicycles; but we still drew the astonished stares to which all foreigners in China, as in much of the Third World, soon become accustomed. Many people find this unbearably oppressive and the lack of privacy is certainly wearing. I have found that a good way to combat it is to decide to be mildly eccentric so that the stares can be rationalized as a natural response rather than the manifest doubting of one's very humanity, which these mass inspections often seem to be. The Chinese, due to a combination of long isolation and powerful independence, suffer to a greater degree than most from cultural and racial arrogance. Foreigners have always been uncivilized hairy barbarians, barely-human foreign devils. This attitude was reinforced for many years after 'Liberation', the communist victory in 1949, by the active xenophobia of party propaganda which emphasized the evils of capitalism while at the same time criticizing the 'revisionist' path of other communist countries, notably Russia.

Jogging is a good way of breaking oneself in to the eccentric approach, since few joggers are seen in China, especially in winter. I relished the prospect of the sensation we would create on horses. I suggested we run along one of the nearby canals instead of down the crowded main boulevards, where there was a real danger of being hit by the already dense early morning bicycle traffic. The moment we turned on to the towpath we seemed to be in the rural China I had read so much about but not yet experienced. There was a grove of pollarded willow trees, thin ice on the water's surface, a lock gate and then a narrow dried mud path twisting between old houses built round courtyards. We glimpsed tiny patches of garden, piles of straw where chickens and pigs scratched and rooted, old women bent over smoking stoves, neat stacks of firewood and husks of corn. Beyond lay some open paddy fields, this close to the very heart of the city. Diplomats who had served in China shortly after the war had told me that then much of the countryside beyond the old city walls was still completely rural, but I had not expected to find so much still there between the highrise buildings.

As we trotted happily along chatting about the day's programme of meetings, our nostrils were suddenly assailed by the most pungent odour imaginable. We passed a night soil storage pit, holding our breath as long as possible. Later we agreed that it was good to see that even here in the capital the famous Chinese thrift, which extends as far as the use of all human waste, was still being practised. Nevertheless we chose a slightly different route on subsequent mornings.

I also hired a bicycle and began to explore Peking on that, finding it far the most sensible form of transport, in spite of the cheapness of taxis. Pedalling along in a crowd of purposeful Chinese was fun. There was also a great freedom to it, as I began to realize through getting lost. Much of Peking still consists of narrow hutungs or lanes where whole communities live behind protecting walls, virtually isolated from the big city around them. While it is impossible to enter these crowded secret areas in a vehicle, it is easy on a bicycle and there I began to experience the taste and feel of China. From the squalor of inconceivably crowded hovels, where smoky charcoal briquettes are made and used for cooking, where refuse is piled up and hurled into the lanes as it used to be in medieval Europe and where glimpses into occasional eating houses reveal interiors reminiscent of Hogarthian gin taverns, emerge people whose clothes are neat and clean and who are clearly setting off to work in an office. Closer inspection shows that the whole set-up is, perforce, extremely efficient.

The keeping of cats and dogs in cities was made illegal some years ago, because they ate too much food and were thought to constitute a disease risk. As a result there are no messes to avoid and no scavengers. Refuse is collected, as is night soil; water is laid on, albeit usually cold, and life is clearly tolerable. The thing which surprised me most and which Mickey said was noticeably different even since his last recent visit was the almost palpable cheerfulness. The horrors of the Cultural Revolution had been halted and reversed in the last few years and the cautious release of steam seemed to be increasing daily. I began to

see the Chinese as a naturally ebullient and jolly people, rather than
the dour ideologues they have seemed since Liberation. The raucous
cries, shrieks of laughter, heated arguments and loud conversations
reminded me far more of a Mediterranean fishing village than an Iron
Curtain country. I was at the time reading Peter Fleming's hilarious
classic on China, *One's Company*, in which he says that 'a sense of
humour, a quickness of perception and a charm of manner . . . were
the best possible qualifications for understanding the Chinese'. These
are not the qualities which other writers had indicated would be
useful. They had only mentioned the Chinese sense of farce and their
disconcerting way of laughing at all embarrassing, painful or shameful
situations. Watching these cheerful people so clearly enjoying the taste
of freedom which the new liberal policy was allowing them, I began to
hope that if we could break through the imaginary screen which, like
the Emperor's clothes, seems to surround foreigners in Chinese eyes,
then we might have an entertaining time among them. Perhaps being
mounted on horses might do the trick.

Meanwhile there remained the problem of breaking through the
real barrier of official resistance to our plans. Robbie had been
working on this and had come up with an idea: 'You need a patron'.

His own most influential friend was Mr Rong Yiren, one of the most
powerful men in China, with whom and through whom he had
already done a lot of useful business. Widely regarded as the man who
has done most to bring about China's economic recovery since the
Cultural Revolution, he was Executive Vice-Chairman of the Standing
Committee of the National People's Congress, Chairman of the China
International Trust & Investment Corporation (CITIC) and China
International Economic Consultants (CIEC) and many other bodies.
Robbie's father, Rob Lyle, had also arrived in Peking partly to
experiment with Chinese cures for Parkinson's disease, from which he
suffered, and partly to negotiate a major joint farming venture. It was
decided that Rob and I would host together a banquet for Mr Rong
Yiren. The quality and opulence of a banquet is directly related to the
difficulty and significance of the matter on which the host seeks his
guests' help. Since Rob was attempting to arrange the first joint
venture in which a foreigner would actually run a farm in China – and
everyone knew that what I was asking was impossible – then nothing
but the best would do.

On the western edge of Peking lies a beautiful garden of lakes and
ponds, through which a river runs. There in the twelfth century the
Emperor Zhang Zong had a fishing lodge erected, which has since
become the central feature of what is now the Daioyutai State Guest-
house. Robbie had received permission for us to hold our banquet in
the fishing lodge. This was a great honour, for which we would pay an
equally great bill.

We arrived in one of the Red Flag limousines used by senior party officials. These huge black cars, only 200 of which are made in China each year in a style unchanged since the 1950s, have plush seats, darkened windows and, for added anonymity, lace curtains. We had to send in advance the registration numbers of all our guests' cars, but we were still stopped and carefully checked by the armed guards at the gate. We drove along tree-lined avenues and over marble bridges past large dark mansions until we reached the fishing lodge. Here coloured lanterns greeted us, discreetly helped by floodlights, which lit our way over a little white bridge and into an ancient courtyard. Gnarled old trees grew from the paving stones, cloisonné urns decorated a terrace between red lacquer pillars and a venerable bronze bell. Inside, priceless treasures rescued from the ravages of this century's successive revolutions were presented casually as they should be, rather than being displayed in dusty glass cases. An immaculate linen table cloth, fine china, silver and glass decorated our banqueting table, but first we went into the parlour to greet our guests. However grand, these reception rooms all adhere to the same pattern throughout China. Armchairs and sofas embellished with lace antimacassars are arranged four square around the walls. The host and chief guest sit at one side and everyone listens to their conversation. It makes for rather stilted chitchat, but fortunately Rob Lyle, as the senior host, made the running and he is masterful at this sort of thing. Mr Rong was a most impressive figure. Large and robust, he looked younger than his sixty-nine years. Formidable at first, he mellowed in response to Rob's wit and by the time we went in to dinner everyone was laughing.

When my turn came to speak I explained why I believed our journey would contribute to the goodwill between our two countries and finished by presenting Mr Rong with a copy of *White Horses*, while asking him if he would be our patron. The general feeling was that the evening had been a complete success and a sound investment. From now on things should get easier.

However, I was still worried sleepless by the fact that nothing tangible had been achieved. Since it was now clear that actual permission to make the ride was going to be a cliffhanger until the last minute, the one thing I might be able to do was to find the horses we would use. It was impossible to find out anything on the subject of horses in Peking and so I went to the place where the Wall begins, Shanhaiguan, 200 miles away, trusting in my Irish luck that something would turn up. A charming young lawyer from CITIC, Mr Hou, agreed to come with me and act as interpreter. But before we could go we had to buy our train tickets, since this has to be done the day before departure.

We made our way to the fine central railway station, one of the best examples of monumental architecture in Peking. Presumably built by the Russians during their heyday here in the 1950s it has two big clock towers (which show the right time) and a huge reception hall with moving staircases. It looks as though it could cope efficiently with any number of people, but fails to do so for two reasons. One is the staggering number of people who use the station. At all hours of the day and night it is crowded to overflowing with people hurrying about. All over the pavements and car parks outside groups of travellers from the far corners of China huddle by their piled up belongings, looking confused as they wait for something to happen. The other ingredient of the chaos is the appalling ingrained bureaucracy of China, which causes even the most simple operation, such as the purchase of a ticket, to be surrounded by almost insuperable rules and regulations.

Foreigners have a special echoing elegant booking hall where life should run smoothly. One has only to enter and see the dejected cluster of backpackers peering at incomprehensible bits of paper on hard seats between great banks of wilting chrysanthemums to see that it does not.

Timetables were unobtainable, but there was a large wall chart of the principal trains each day. It only showed the trains' ultimate destination and so it was necessary to consult a map of China in order to work out if a certain train might stop at the station of one's choice. We worked it out and queued at the only tiny pigeon hole being manned. When our turn came we could see a cross-looking girl sitting sideways and ignoring us.

'Excuse me,' said Mr Hou. 'Could we have two tickets, soft class, to Shanhaiguan on the 8.40 a.m. train tomorrow?'

With a toss of her head and without looking up, she replied, 'Mei you!' This literally means 'not have' and is the instinctive initial response, it seems, to all questions addressed to officials and shop assistants in China by foreigners and Chinese people alike. There seems to be a general feeling that service with a smile is somehow degrading and bourgeois.

'How about hard class?' I made Mr Hou ask. She shook her head as though he had asked for a special coach. 'The early train?' I suggested, since we were both quite ready to make a 5 a.m. start. Again a firm no, and so it went on as we tried trains and classes throughout the day. The queue behind us became restless as she shuffled tickets and money busily and did her best to pretend we were not there. As we were patiently working through the afternoon trains she suddenly lost interest in the game and thrust two tickets and other vital bits of paper through the slot. They were soft class tickets for the train we had originally requested and cost about £3 each for the 200 mile journey.

Once we had fought our way through the morning throng to our train, our own comfortable sleeping compartment was a delight.

Mr Hou reading *White Horses Over France* in our sleeping compartment on the way to Shanhaiguan.

There were four bunk beds draped with white sheets embroidered with blue flowers, a table with lace tablecloth, lamp and pretty pink lampshade, a real begonia in a decorated brown pot and a television set mounted on the wall. Grey velvet curtains with muslin netting behind screened the window and there were hooks to hang our coats from as well as a thermos of hot water for making tea. There was even a thermometer on the wall and the heating was full on. Less desirable were a loudspeaker through which for the first twenty minutes a strident girl's voice instructed the passengers what they were not allowed to have on board, such as explosives, and two Greek sailors, who lay in the top bunks smoking when awake and snoring resonantly when asleep. But I had my Walkman and a stock of Mozart tapes, which I always take on trains to cut out distractions, and at last I was travelling through the Chinese countryside. I played a childhood game of pretending I was on a horse cantering beside the train, leaping over obstructions as they loomed up. It seemed good riding country with lots of dirt roads and cart tracks leading off to the horizon between rows of poplars. I began to dream about being free to travel out into this country.

One of the best books about China is *The Middle Kingdom* by Erwin Wickert. In it he describes perfectly what I was after:

Insulated from the desert by the windows of our car, we could only guess at the sensation which so many travellers had sought to conjure up in print and paint, only to find that its true essence eluded them. I myself, who had experienced the indescribable in other deserts, could not have defined it.

A long way from the road, a man was riding a camel with another camel trotting riderless behind. He must have been heading for some destination, presumably along a track which only he could discern in the endless, stony waste, but to us in our motorized cage he seemed bound for nowhere from nowhere. I envied the man. What, I wondered, would it be like to get out and accompany him on the second camel? Uncomfortable, certainly. The saddle-cloth would be infested with fleas, and the most I would get for supper would be flat cakes of bread and cold mutton fat. But we would ride off into infinity, and at some stage, perhaps, if only for an instant while swaying along or resting when we halted for the night, I might experience the Unio Mystica, that great and all-embracing unity of which the Chinese Taoists also spoke. Such are the fleeting moments for which a person should live – the moments when he becomes a True Man . . .

One of the great pleasures of train travel in China is the large number of fine great steam engines to be seen. Although our own train was pulled by diesel, I saw them in every station and siding puffing clouds of black smoke while white steam escaped between their great wheels. The drivers waved cheerfully when they saw me peering out at them, as did the jolly red-faced girls in brightly coloured padded jackets working on the track. A shepherd grazed his flock of sheep on the embankment and we passed a herd of very pink pigs who stopped their rooting and rushed off at the sound of the train.

It was very exciting to see the countryside and the regularly spaced villages, still partly screened by the willows and poplars losing the last of their autumn leaves. As I gazed I tried to imagine what life was like

Farming in the Hebei plain. Heaps of manure are being spread by hand, while a donkey pulls a harrow.

A mule almost buried under a heavy load of straw.

for the people I could see riding on their carts behind mules, horses and donkeys, or trudging along under heavy loads. The villages consisted of row after row of identical bungalows looking a bit like railway carriages with the wheels removed and I missed the relief and focal point of a church, mosque or temple. The only imposing buildings, ancient or modern, which I saw on the long journey across the Hebei plain were great factories, whose rows of tall chimneys spewed their message to the heavens. They are the temples of modern China.

On arrival in Shanhaiguan a cheerful, round-faced policeman at the station offered to find us the only taxi and then decided to come with us. Mr Hou explained what we were there for and a general discussion followed with much shaking of heads over the prospect of finding riding horses, but an enthusiastic willingness to help us in our quest. I had to admit that I had not seen a single person riding a horse on the whole seven-hour journey.

We drove to see the Great Wall. The old town lies up against the Wall and most of its own walls are intact, with narrow gateways leading to the crowded streets beyond. The magnificent east gate has been restored and bears the inscription 'The First Pass Under Heaven' in huge characters on the double-roofed tower. Beyond lies the province of Liaoning, part of old Manchuria, which for 2,000 years was peopled by barbarian Tartars who constantly threatened China's peace.

Up on the Wall it was bitterly cold with an icy wind blowing off the mountains to the north west. It was almost unbearably exciting to see the Wall winding up from the coastal plain into those mountains like a great grey snake and knowing that it continued westwards for another 2,000 miles (3219 kilometres) to the last fort at Jiayuguan where we hoped to end our ride. Below the gate I found a notice in Chinese and English:

JOINT PROPOSAL FOR RESTORATION OF SHANHAIGUAN GREAT WALL

A popular saying goes, 'Shanhaiguan is unmatched as a unique lock for two capitals. It's the First Pass Under Heaven.' It is by the laudatory appellation of 'The First Pass Under Heaven' that the Shanhaiguan Great Wall is renowned throughout the world.

The Shanhaiguan Great Wall slopes down along the ridges of Yanshan Mountains in Hebei Province and then rises and falls across a series of mountain ranges until it finally plunges straight into the Bohai Sea. Here, the breath-taking shan (mountain), hai (sea), and guan (pass) possess the majesty of a crouching tiger and a coiling dragon. No wonder the grandiose Shanhaiguan with its strategic significance can best represent the beauty and strength of the Chinese nation and is considered one of the most important sections of the world wonder Great Wall.

We, representatives of 39 units throughout China, have responded to Comrade Deng Xiaoping's call, 'Love our motherland and repair the Great Wall.' At the invitation of the China Shanhaiguan Great Wall Research Institute we recently made an inspection of this vicinity. It was with great distress and sorrow that we viewed Shanhaiguan in its present dilapidated state. Originally this section of the Great Wall stretched for 23.85 km; now only 8.45 km of it is left. Once there were 34 watch towers, but only 14 remain. Of the 10 main passes built in the past, only 3 can be found. It is especially painful to us that the 'old dragon head', a 23.3 metre long and 10 metre high extension of the Great Wall which protrudes into the sea, has never been repaired since its destruction by the Eight Power Allied Forces in 1900. The ten thousand li long dragon still lacks its head.

As we look at Shanhaiguan Great Wall now we are aware that if the head of this great dragon is not restored in our time, we will stand shamefaced before our ancestors, our descendants and the whole human civilization. How can we sons and daughters of China or overseas Chinese stand aloof or remain apathetic in this regard. With this in mind we jointly propose to the whole society:

1. Take positive action in response to Comrade Deng Xiaoping's call, 'Love our motherland and repair the Great Wall.' We welcome compatriots at home and abroad and overseas Chinese to offer their suggestions and make donations of money and effort for restoration work on Shanhaiguan Great Wall, a treasure of human civilization. We also warmly welcome donations and contributions from foreign friends.

2. While the project will be mainly financed by the state, we call for organization of all kinds of social activities, benefit shows and sports meets,

etc to solicit contributions from collectives and individuals. We also call upon enterprises to make investments.

3. We unanimously agree that, as expressions of thanks and in way of commemoration, donators who contribute 5 yuan or more will have their names signed in the 'Love our motherland and repair the Great Wall' autograph album, which shall be kept as a cultural relic in the Shanhaiguan Great Wall Museum; bronze, silver or gold Great Wall medals will be awarded donators who contribute 10 yuan or more; individuals who contri-

'The First Pass Under Heaven' at Shanhaiguan. The Research Institute is on the left and a new building will soon obscure this view.

bute 100 yuan or more and units which contribute 1,000 yuan or more will have their names engraved on tablets; individuals that donate huge sums for the restoration of a particular section of the Great Wall will have a big tablet or a pavilion erected for them in the said site in commemoration. These tablets or pavilions will be forever preserved as historic relics alongside the Great Wall.

The Great Wall is awaiting!

There then followed a list of sponsoring organizations in China.

Mr Hou and I went to call on the Shanhaiguan Great Wall Research Institute, which was housed in a pleasant building in the square next to

the gate. We were well received, enthusiastically when I said I hoped our ride might raise some money for restoring the Wall. I made a donation to their work, in return for which I was presented with a gold plated badge of the First Pass. They told us that three young men from Shanhaiguan had recently returned from walking along the Wall to Jiayuguan, taking 500 days to do so. They said they were ordinary workers who had undertaken the journey without sponsorship but had simply relied on the help of friendly people and officials along the way. We asked if we could meet them, but were told that they were now in Liaoning Province walking the 'Willow Wall' to Dandong on the border of North Korea. This palisade or 'pale' was a fence made out of elm and willow trees and it was originally erected in the eleventh century by the Song rulers to keep out the Khitans, wild horsemen from the north who, like all the other northern non-Chinese people, lived beyond the pale.

The Khitans, whose name was corrupted to Cathay, were brilliant horsemen, using teams of mounted archers to conquer their enemies. These were called 'ordos', from which came the word 'hordes' when Ghengis Khan used a similar system to sweep westward into Europe. They developed a strong agricultural nation and built their own walls to keep the Song out.

Mr Hou and I spent the night in the big nearby port of Qinhuangdao as we were told (wrongly as it turned out) that there were no hotels in Shanhaiguan. In the morning our friendly policeman informed us he had had a brainwave. He thought the army might have some horses and so we drove straight to the local barracks. It was a huge rambling place with bleak buildings between areas of hard brown earth where an icy wind blew through occasional basketball posts and cold soldiers, often barefoot, wandered about in shabby uniforms. They all seemed to have the same rank but one was eventually identified as 'Chief of Staff'. He said that we could go and see the horses. He also said there were eight of them, but when we arrived at the stables we found that five of the animals tied up under a tin-roofed shelter were mules. Of the remaining three one was clearly hopeless, being lame, far too small and vicious; it tried to bite me as soon as I approached. I began to examine the two remaining possibles, trying to look as knowledgeable and confident as possible.

Before leaving Cornwall I had asked our local vet to instruct me in the complicated art of telling a horse's age from its teeth. He had explained carefully about measurements, lengths and grooves but most of it had been above my head or too subtle to be easily remembered. Only one piece of information had stuck. This was that at about six years old a slight hook or 'cusp' appears at the side of the tooth and that it disappears at about eight. There was a chestnut gelding which looked quite big and strong compared with its companion, so I felt its legs for lumps, stroked its neck, which it did not seem to mind and had a look at its teeth. I was really only doing so to see if they were all there and in order to look intelligent, but like a flash of light I saw it – a cuspid hook! As nonchalantly as I could I turned to Mr Hou and said, 'This one's about seven years old, I see.' The Chief of Staff, when Mr Hou had translated this to him, called over one of the soldiers responsible for the horses and asked him a question. At his reply, which I gathered confirmed my assessment, I could feel my status rise with the company, but the hardest part was yet to come. I asked if I could try out the chestnut and it was saddled up. Chinese army saddles are well made and quite comfortable, but they perch high on the horse's back leaving little to hang on to. I had been spoiled for the last year or so by riding in my deep, comfortable Camargue saddle and was not looking forward to mounting what they warned me was quite a lively animal. The yard was rough and stony; I did not want to fall off and lose a lot of face as well as injure myself. All at once the whole idea of riding across China seemed less appealing. The likelihood of one of us falling off at some stage and having to be taken to hospital seemed high, and Chinese hospitals do not have a very good reputation. There was no turning back, however, so I gingerly climbed aboard, at which the horse gave a series of little bucks and began to head back towards his friends. It was difficult to make him do anything else, as he failed to respond to the usual signals. Also one of the mules had broken loose and kept rushing up to try and kick us. While I struggled to trot and walk round the yard one of the soldiers mounted the remaining pony, which was black and rather hairy. As soon as he was on he walloped it into a canter and began to career around. Everyone shouted that I should follow him and so we took off out of the yard and down a rough avenue towards the main buildings. This I guessed was the normal exercise run for the horses and it seemed that it was always done flat out. My horse seemed happier at this speed and bucked less often, so I hung on and followed the soldier who whooped wildly and led the way around the barracks. Back in the yard I tried out the black, which was a much nicer ride, though quite a bit smaller, and I decided that it would suit Louella well as she is about two stone lighter than I am. When I later measured them I found the chestnut gelding to be 14.3 hands and the black, also a gelding, 13.1.

Back in the main barrack building we climbed stained stone staircases and went along bare dusty corridors past broken windows and scruffy rooms with iron bedsteads to what I assumed was the Officers' Mess. There were blue plastic coated armchairs around the walls and a bunch of artificial flowers in a vase. On the walls were pictures of Victorian ladies and children in crinolines. A jolly quartermaster plied us with tea from a thermos saying 'good day' and 'goodbye' in English as he poured. Then the Colonel arrived. There was no mistaking him.

He wore badges of rank, unlike every other soldier I had seen so far, and a neatly pressed uniform instead of sagging fatigues. We explained our needs and he took it all in instantly.

'You should have come two weeks ago,' he said. 'I had to sell off eleven horses then and there would have been no problem in selling them to you.'

I asked how much he'd got for them and he told me that they had averaged about 700 yuan each. I said that this was just the sort of money I was looking to pay and offered to buy the two I had just ridden.

'The trouble is,' he replied, 'these ones are officially members of the People's Army and I cannot dispose of them without permission from higher authority.' Fortunately, someone who had the authority to authorize the sale, General Zhou, was due to arrive the next day on an inspection visit.

Mr Hou and I at once wrote a polite letter to the General requesting permission to buy the horses, explaining what I planned to do with them and presenting him with the copy of *White Horses* which had already been shown round all those present as explanation of Louella's and my crazy desire to ride across countries rather than go by bus. Everyone agreed that this should do the trick, and the Colonel promised to look after the horses well until our return in the following April. I offered the company a carton of Marlboro cigarettes I had bought on the aeroplane for just such an occasion, but they were vehemently refused and I thought I might have caused offence, even though everyone had smoked constantly throughout our meeting. Then I suggested that they might share them with the General tomorrow and they were accepted with glee all round. I made a little speech complimenting them on the condition of their horses and asking if it could be maintained during the next five months. I thanked them for their hospitality and kindness, declined an invitation to lunch and left suppressing whoops of joy with difficulty. It looked as though we had cracked one of the three problems which might make the ride impossible and proved wrong all those who had said we would not find horses in China.

In a state of euphoria I suggested to Mr Hou that we should now relax and enjoy ourselves as tourists. He was as pleased as I was and our policeman and taxi driver had caught the mood, so that we were a very merry party. We decided to visit the Jiangnu Temple about four miles to the east. Here there is a statue to a legendary lady called Meng Jiang who has been venerated for more than 2,000 years. Her husband was one of the innumerable people conscripted to build the original Wall by the Emperor Qin in the third century BC. Worried that he might be cold she travelled thousands of miles in search of him, carrying warm clothing. At last she reached a spot where she was told

'At the foot of the temple steps was a white horse which gave me a strong sense of *déjà vu*.'

he had died from the hard labour. Her tears melted the Wall and the bones of her husband, who like many others had been used as ballast in its building, popped out into her arms. Carrying them back to Shanhaiguan she threw herself into the sea with them.

At the foot of the temple steps was a white horse which gave me a strange sense of *déjà vu*. In the first place I had had it vaguely in mind that we would make this ride, too, on white horses. Then there is another legend that the Emperor Qin himself rode on a white horse, which could fly with its legs as well as if it had wings and which used to appear to the builders and show them where the Wall should be built. One foggy day they lost sight of it, but continued to build in the same direction. When the fog cleared weeks later, they saw the horse far off to the side and so had to go back and start again. This is said to account for the spurs and false loops of the Wall. They say the white horse is still seen sometimes near the Wall in wild and misty weather. Now here was the very horse, caparisoned in red and available for tourists to be photographed sitting on.

Although much bigger than the two I had just seen, even I could tell it was a great age, had rotten feet and was not designed for long distance travel. However, just for fun I asked how much it would cost, as I posed obligingly in the saddle for my companions. 'White horse cost 1000 yuan [about £200] but not sell,' was the reply.

We climbed up to the temple where there is a fine view of the Wall and the mountains from the Waiting for Husband Rock where Meng Jiang is supposed to have sat and looked out for her husband. I bought a postcard of it to send to Louella and we drove to see Old Dragon Head, the place where the Wall actually starts on the edge of the Bohai Sea. The Wall was seen as a dragon by the Chinese, its head drinking from the sea, its tail far inland, its body coiled along the mountains. In China the dragon is a symbol of strength and energy, an auspicious presence, not a destructive one as in the West. There was no recognized way of approaching this spot and I had been warned that it was a military zone closed to foreigners. As we approached the sea we came to a barrier across the track, guarded by a soldier. At first he would not let our taxi through, but when we explained that I was a foreign tourist and only interested in seeing the Great Wall, he waved us on. We found ourselves in a large army camp with rows of huts, soldiers marching about and, above our heads, huge radar antennae rotating. It clearly was a rather sensitive place, a listening post of China's eastern defences perhaps, and I felt sure we would be kicked out soon. Trying to look as official as possible we scrambled over the ridge separating us from the shore and emerged onto a pleasant rocky beach.

The Wall at its very end had crumbled away. Only a few large cut rocks in the sea marked the point where the final buttress must have stood in the waves. They were once joined together with molten iron poured into grooves, which were still visible. Here in 1900 a British force landed to attack Shanhaiguan from the sea, burning down a nearby town and seizing the fort and barracks behind us as their headquarters. Now I could see that the end section of the Wall, which ran northwards along the beach, was being restored and it looked as though the whole place was about to be developed into a tourist resort. Well, I thought, if the British had played their part in knocking it down, the least I could do was to try and raise some money towards its rebuilding.

We picked our way along the icy foreshore and climbed back into the camp, while I blithely snapped away at everything in sight. Nobody seemed to mind until, as we were crossing the barrack square, I noticed that one of the inevitable netball posts was propped up by a millstone exactly like the one I have as a front door step at home in Cornwall. When I stopped to photograph this shouts of protest were raised and, surprised, we fled. It was only when the picture was developed back in England that I realized that framed between the posts was one of the radar installations.

On the way back to Peking I asked Mr Hou if he might be able to come with us as our interpreter. His English was so good and he had such a nice sense of humour that I felt sure we would all get on. Aged twenty-eight, he had been married for six months but, like so many others in China, was only able to see his wife once or twice a year. She was a doctor and lived in his home town of Qingdao in Shandong province. He had done his legal training in Canton and I had been impressed by the way he had represented my unlikely case when negotiating with the army over the horses.

I asked him to help choose suitable Chinese names for us. Our full names are quite impossible for general use in China where almost all names consist of only two or three syllables, the first being the surname. Due to the complexities of Chinese, subtle tone or pronunciation differences will produce a totally different meaning and so the choices of name, starting from a European root, are almost infinite. We started with my name. He asked me which three syllables I would like to use. 'I thought perhaps the Han from Hanbury, followed by Robin,' I suggested. 'Let's see,' he replied. 'Han is fine. It's about the commonest Chinese name, like Smith, so we need do nothing with that. But Robin does not mean anything in Chinese and will be hard for people to pronounce or remember. I will have to work on it.' For half an hour or so he tried out sounds and meanings, mouthing Ro, Lo, Wo and other strange noises while at the same time scribbling characters. At last he said, 'One of the meanings of Lo can be "happy". Would you say you are a happy person?'

'Very much so,' I answered.

'Then if you use Bin to mean guest you would be Happy Guest Han. How about that?'

'Perfect,' I said. Much later I was to learn that Lo Bin can also mean pancake, which I found less appropriate, but Louella seemed to find funny.

It was then her turn. 'This is harder,' said Mr Hou, 'as the sounds are less familiar.'

Since husbands and wives do not have the same surnames in China, we settled for Louella as her three syllables. 'Once again Lou is easy,' said Mr Hou. 'It's another common surname, but "Ella" is going to be harder.' After a while he asked if she liked babies and I replied that she was mad about them, having just had her third. 'Then how about Er Wa?' he said. 'That means Love Baby.' And so she became Love Baby Lou.

I had my revenge for her mirth at my pancake tag when, on our way out through Hong Kong, someone at a dinner party nearly fell out of his chair on being told proudly by Louella the Chinese name she had been given. 'Love Baby has quite a different connotation here from the one you think!' he said, adding that it meant 'Girl for the use of loving'.

2

BATTLES WITH
BUREAUCRACY

A lmost exactly five months later, I returned to Shanhaiguan, this time with Louella as well as Mr Hou. We had flown out to Peking a couple of weeks before and, while all our other plans still looked extremely shaky, we wanted at least to be sure of the horses. This time we were taken to a delightful old mansion in the walled city and in sight of the First Pass, which had just been converted into a most comfortable small hotel. It was once, we were told, the late Defence Minister Marshal Lin Biao's house. We were given his old bedroom, No. 1, unchanged since the day in September 1971 when he was killed in an air crash in Mongolia. His departure from the Chinese political scene is shrouded in mystery. Just two years after being named as Mao's successor and 'closest comrade in arms' he was branded as having plotted to assassinate the Chairman and usurp all power. Whether he was himself murdered or whether the plane in which he was fleeing the country (a British-made Trident, incidentally) crashed or was shot down may never be known.

Whatever happened then, we benefited from the fact that his house, one of several he was said to have owned in the area, had been preserved. There was a deep iron bath on legs with plenty of hot water for an hour or so in the evening – a rare luxury in rural China – and two big hard double beds in our room. It was divided by a carved wooden screen and there were comfortable old arm chairs and even a refrigerator in the sitting area. We were to get to know that room quite well.

In Shanhaiguan's splendid old lime green taxi, made in Russia in 1950, we entered the army barracks in style. We had sent a cable saying we were on our way to collect and pay for the horses but had, of course, received no reply and now had our fingers crossed that they would still be there. At first it looked bad. A new unit had just taken over and were in the process of moving in so that no one knew what was going on. There were field guns wrapped in canvas covers parked in rows on the parade ground, their barrels pointing to the sky. We felt we should not be seeing them and resisted the temptation to take photographs. The stable area seemed deserted and we peered hopelessly through blackened windows into the derelict buildings. Then we saw something move and were able to make out two horses in the dim interior. It seemed that our cable had arrived in the nick of time. The two horses I had chosen in November had been left behind with two soldiers to look after them. Their saddles and bridles were there too, they had been freshly shod and looked in fairly good shape. We rode them and mine bucked as before, while Louella's small black one kicked out at everyone around. But we managed to stay on and even repeated the circuit of the barracks at a canter, allowing them to choose the route.

There was, of course, no question of our turning them down now, since we had no alternatives, so that when the new Colonel appeared we would have had to agree to any price he demanded. The instructions he had been left by his predecessor were quite clear. Although the horses had originally cost 1500 yuan each in Mongolia, we were to be charged 800 yuan each plus another 200 yuan in total for their tack and keep. 'General Zhou said you were to be treated fairly and, besides, the People's Army is not a commercial organization,' he told us. Since this came in total to less than £200 for each fully equipped horse, we paid up happily and took formal possession of them. We blew into their nostrils in the prescribed Barbara Woodhouse manner so as to imprint our scent on them (this surprised both them and the onlooking soldiers) and named them Tang and Ming. At least one problem was now resolved. We still had many things to sort out back in Peking but we hoped that a week or so would take care of that. We left saying we would return soon, and that meanwhile we hoped the soldiers would give Tang and Ming lots of exercise each day.

Since our train back to Peking did not leave until midday the next day, we decided to get up early and walk as far inland along the Wall as we could. Shanhaiguan, which means the pass between the mountains and the sea, has always been of critical strategic significance to China. The original gate was built in AD 618, the first year of the Tang dynasty, while the present one was built under the Ming in 1639. Thus Tang and Ming turned out to be quite appropriate names for our first horses.

The first few miles of the Great Wall at Shanhaiguan are among the finest and most elaborate sections along its entire length. The walls at the very start are 46 feet (14 metres) high and 23 feet (7 metres) thick, as opposed to the relatively modest Wall at Badaling visited by every tourist, which is 26 feet (7.8 metres) high and 19 feet (5.8 metres) wide. It was made here of bricks laid on great granite slabs with rammed earth inside and it was perhaps the most important defensive stretch of all. It protected the narrow plain between the mountains and the sea; any invading army getting past was home and dry in China.

Treachery by the General in charge in 1644 led directly to the downfall of the Ming dynasty and the start of Manchu rule. Since then it has been known as Traitor's Gate.

It is often said that the Wall is wide enough for five or six horsemen to ride abreast and in places this is true. But it is unlikely that horses were often taken up onto the ramparts as the passages through the numerous watch towers were too narrow for horses to pass. There were frequent flights of steps and, for the first few hundred miles of Wall at least, many sections are far too steep for a horse to climb. There are said to be 25,000 watch towers along the Wall and in places they are very close together. It did, however, serve as an elevated highway for messengers and footsoldiers who could rush to defend threatened sections. Messengers were also sent rapidly over great distances between strategically placed beacon towers. Fires of wolves' dung were lit, as the smoke from these apparently flows straight upwards and so makes signalling easier. One column of smoke and a single gunshot (gunpowder was invented in China in the eighth century) represented an enemy force of about 100, two of each 500, three 1,000 and five columns and shots meant 5,000 were attacking. These were the rules laid down by the emperor in 1466.

We set off briskly inland along the top of the Wall from the gate, only to be stopped by a barbed wire fence after 100 yards. This we climbed over, but we soon had to give up. At the point where the Wall separated from the old town walls of Shanhaiguan there was a wide gap. We had to scramble down into the town and leave by the north gate. A rough road ran towards the mountains parallel to the Wall and we followed this. On our right the inner, mud face of the Wall was eroded and overgrown, while on the outer side beyond, most of the stone facing was impressively intact. Just before it started to climb we crossed to the outer side and came upon a delightful rustic scene. A family of peasants in colourful clothes was ploughing behind a mule. Even the youngest child was working away, busily wielding a large spade to good effect. We climbed from here along the top of the Wall. It soon became very steep with a narrow paved surface and a crenallated outer edge. There was only room for one person at a time and as the slope of the hill fell away below us I, who am a coward about heights, began to feel a touch of vertigo. Louella and Mr Hou, in his unsuitable city shoes, were braver and forged ahead to come to a stop against a cliff face below the first beacon tower. Here we could go no further without returning to the bottom and detouring around the side of the hill to pick up the Wall again above the cliff. In this immediate way we found that the Great Wall is not and never was actually continuous. Natural features were used where a wall was unnecessary. We sat and gazed out over the spectacular view to the south across the plain, the walled town and the sea beyond, where many large freigh-

Watch-towers along the Wall often stretch from horizon to horizon.

ters and tankers were steaming past to and from Qinhuangdao. This was once one of the northernmost Treaty Ports, where foreigners were allowed to reside, carry on business and own land. Now it is a highly polluted industrial city, the end of an oil pipeline and an important ice-free port. We could see the smoke of its chimneys.

In the shelter of the Wall it was quite hot and the sun shone, but a chill wind blew off the hills. The scenery around us was alpine, pretty as a postcard with scattered fir trees under which grazed flocks of white goats, while brown cows grazed on the grassy slopes. The sounds of the plain were carried up to us; voices, bleats and tinkling bells with only the occasional putt-putt of a mini tractor. We returned along the outer side of the Wall, passing an old man pulling a stone roller in a wrought iron frame behind him along the rows of corn; then into the medieval lanes of the old external town, where we bought some hot muffins at a stall. They were made of white flour and coated with millet seeds before being baked on the outside. Delicious and 10 fen (2p) each.

Delicious food being cooked at a village stall.

Louella and Mr Hou returning from walking inland along the Wall from
Shanhaiguan.

The telexes which we had exchanged with our various host organizations before we left England had become increasingly discourag-
ing as the time for our departure had neared. 'We would be much
grateful if yu can postpone to next year,' said one. 'We are a profit
seeking company. We understand yr project has a strong background
to promote friendship. We prefer not to be involved in your project.'
This was a prelude to a suggestion that we pay a fee of £250,000 for
the necessary arrangements to be made. At this point I made my first
appeal, by telex, to our patron Mr Rong, asking if such a sum were
really unavoidable for a ride which was being undertaken for charity.
Suddenly there was no fee and at the last moment, long after we had in
fact arranged to do so, we were invited to come to Peking to discuss
matters. When I telexed our arrival date and said we would need some
help with customs clearance, a frantic telex came back telling us not to
bring anything with us, as we were simply expected for further
discussions at this stage, conveniently failed to reach us. The reason
that we anticipated problems at the Peking customs was that we did
have a great deal with us. We wanted to pre-empt all practical
objections to our ride by having everything necessary with us so we
could be independent if need be, so that we could never be accused of
being a burden on the local population, and the excuse that facilities

for foreigners were not available could not be used against us. Cathay Pacific had most generously made this approach possible for us by agreeing to waive our excess baggage charges. We had a splendid three-compartment tent complete with mosquito nets in which our party could sleep if there were no accommodation. We had already blithely announced to the world that we would be employing a cook and interpreter, as well as a driver for our support vehicle, although we had no idea where we were going to find them.

Dairy Farm had been so generous with food for the journey that reluctantly we had to turn down two thirds of it as the weight would have taxed even Cathay Pacific's goodwill, but we still had enough to feed a small army though we hoped we could live on local produce.

The only other sponsorship we received came from Marconi, whose Marketing Director I met in a farmhouse high on Bodmin Moor and who generously said we must take their most modern walkie-talkie radios with us in case we got lost. That equipment alone comprised three packing cases and a ten foot aerial.

We had brought the wonderfully comfortable saddles on which we had ridden across France – we had no intention of suffering daily in anything else if we could help it. Boots, clothes, cameras, film and forty copies of *White Horses* as presents combined to make up a formidable quantity of baggage; thirty-two pieces in all, weighing in at 600 kilos. The nice thing about having quite so much baggage, we found, is that you are such an obvious nuisance that you receive special treatment and usually end up travelling first class as well. At the Hong Kong check-in counter everything is X-rayed before being allowed on board. Some of our larger trunks would not fit into the machine and had to be inspected by hand. This was done scrupulously and with infinite politeness by a Chinese security man, who removed everything and laid it out in rows on the concourse floor. He found two things which were not allowed on board. One was an aerosol of the invaluable purple antiseptic spray which no stock farmer is ever without; the other was a can of special leather dressing for our saddles. These items were put on one side and Louella and I and the security man forced everything back into the trunks. The situation was so unlikely that for once the flap and fluster of airport life failed to annoy us and we were all polite and good humoured throughout. But I don't like being beaten and as soon as our last items had been cleared and checked in I nipped over to the airport post office and airmailed the two forbidden items to myself in Peking. They arrived safely a week later.

Meanwhile we had the major obstacle ahead of Peking customs. For once we were not met on arrival. Normally visitors to China are met by a representative of their host organization, but we had already managed to blur the issue of who really was our host and, probably wisely, none of those who might have considered themselves responsible for us risked turning up at what was likely to be a stormy occasion. We fully expected all our stuff to be impounded and to have to spend the first week or so getting it cleared. Among the main items forbidden without special permission on the obligatory customs declaration forms are radio transmitters and foodstuffs. We put down our watches and cameras, covering all the rest with the heading 'expedition equipment'. Deciding to try and brazen it out, but with little hope of success, I went over to the row of baggage trolleys and paid for six. One of the nice anomalies facing the traveller arriving in China is that prominent both on entry forms and signs is the warning that it is forbidden to take Chinese currency in or out of the country, yet you cannot get a baggage trolley in the arrival hall without paying. I had learned my lesson the first time round, when I had seen the old hands hurrying forward with notes outstretched. I had also received a first insight into the Chinese way of doing things. Many things seem impossible on the surface, but there is usually a way around.

I persuaded five of the girl porters to take a trolley each and stand by the baggage carousel while Louella and I loaded a couple of heavy items on to each. Leaving Louella to stack up the rest as it arrived, I set off for the single exit, looking as confident as I could and with my five attendants in tow. At that moment a fairy godmother appeared in the form of a beautiful and elegant Chinese girl we had met in London who was returning home to Peking on the same flight. She offered to help. 'These are friends of mine who are going on an expedition,' she said, with a delightful mixture of charm and authority. My form was stamped and we all swept through. Outside in the bedlam of the crowded arrival area I found an empty space on the pavement, unloaded the trolleys, left one girl in charge and shepherded my flock back in. Twice more we loaded up and swept smilingly past the customs counters, the final time with Louella who had been nobly grabbing, stacking and checking our belongings. Everything passed through safely and without question.

A twenty seater minibus was barely able to carry us and all our luggage to the Jianguo Hotel where the kind manager allowed us to take over their store room. For our first few days in Peking I constantly expected to be tapped on the shoulder and told that the customs service wanted a word with me, but gradually I began to accept that we had actually beaten the system. Maybe the rest would also fall into place as we planned.

Being in Peking with Louella was a lot more fun than it had been on my own. We hired bicycles and explored together. We went shopping for the children and visited all the sights. We got up very early and saw the Wall at Badaling before the first tourists arrived and we discovered little restaurants together where we could dine out late with only red paper lanterns between us and the stars. We also made a lot of friends and were entertained most generously. But none of this was what we had come for and we fretted at the delays and the expense.

Meetings were always inconclusive, studded with vague references to 'the relevant authority' and 'the department concerned'. We all knew who was being referred to, but it simply is not done in China to mention the military or the police. We knew that the Wall, running as it does parallel with China's northern border, passes almost entirely through sensitive military areas and that if the military said 'no' there would be no appeal. But we hoped that our constant requests for a decision might force the issue. Also we knew that, thanks to Robbie, people were rooting for us and that there was a general feeling that letting us make the ride would be a 'good thing'. David Griffith's proposed run along the Wall added to the pressure, because if one party could be allowed to go then so could the other. In the end he had to postpone his run as he had just been appointed Managing Director of Wembley Stadium.

Our Embassy was wonderful. In spite of the fact that it was all in a state of considerable upheaval because of the forthcoming state visit by the Queen and Prince Philip, they helped us in all sorts of ways to keep our sanity and achieve our ends. The Information Officer, John Dennis, was detailed to keep a watching brief on us if we did manage to disappear into remote regions. He sat in on several meetings and while he quite properly made it clear that we were in no way official visitors, his very presence gave us an aura of respectability we might otherwise have lacked. Richard and Grania Evans, the Ambassador and his wife, took pity on us when the Jianguo Hotel said they needed our room. They were suffering the worst disruption of all as the Residence was being completely redecorated and they were having to camp with their young children on the top floor. But they had a spare room for us and a large, peaceful garden to enjoy.

One of the strangest things about China at this time was that nobody knew exactly what the law was. While there was officially an 'Open Door' policy, there was also an ingrained fear and suspicion of change. We were learning how hard it was to get permission to make an individual journey, even though everyone seemed agreed in principle that it was a good idea. The same problem applied to the free markets, which had recently sprung up everywhere. Theoretically they were permitted, but every now and then the police would close one down. Especially sensitive were antique markets, where illegal treasures might be offered to tourists. One which had recently been closed and then reopened was at the Bird Market and we went there with Grania Evans. The Chinese love to keep cage birds, especially Hwameis, thrushlike birds which sing constantly like an English blackbird on a spring morning. Their owners exercise them by taking them for walks, swinging their wooden cages up and down to streng-

The Chinese love to keep cage birds, which they take for walks and even bicycle rides, believing that strengthening their legs improves their singing.

then their legs as they cling to their perches. This is said to improve their voices. There were lots of Hwameis in the market and they sounded like a dawn chorus. Hanging in small wooden cages were all sorts of other little birds which we tried to identify later with the help of the Evans's library of bird books. There was a Peking robin, which was bought for the children, siskins, bramblings, and lots of other finches, including greenfinches and a Beautiful Rosefinch. Coal tits, marsh tits and a whole variety of exotic little red billed seed eaters and budgerigars, which I suppose must have been imported at some time, abounded. Saddest of all was a young sparrow hawk wrapped in a cloth and glaring around with angry bright yellow eyes. This, I feared, was more likely to be sold for consumption as a form of medicine than to be trained for falconry.

The 'antiques' were produced rather surreptitiously from among the birds. Mostly it was junk for which high prices were being asked, but after the conformity of state shops it was refreshing to be able to haggle. There were some nice old carved boxes, ceramic plates and bowls, little gourds with carved ivory tops for keeping crickets in and some silver and brass pipes and incense burners. I bought a small silver water pipe because it seemed old and had the Yin and Yang symbols as well as an inscription. Richard Evans later translated this as 'to be used when the bright moon shines between the pine trees and the spring water bubbles over the stones'.

Just when we thought we must be breaking through the bureaucracy, another problem would be thrown at us. After two weeks of negotiations we were beginning to feel caught in a spider's web. Without a single host we presented special problems to the authorities, since much of their concern centred on who would take responsibility for us if anything went wrong on the journey. My assurances that I took full responsibility for everything fell on deaf ears. Without being paid huge sums of money no single organization was prepared to look after us and in any case we had already spread our arrangements too widely for that. Thanks to the Embassy we had been allowed, as a special concession, to recruit our interpreter and cook from the Diplomatic Service Bureau, the staff normally only available to diplomats. Mr Hou was not able to come with us as his wife was having a baby and he had been given permission to join her for the birth. Our support vehicle and driver came through CITIC and we had arranged the horses ourselves. But without an overall host there would be no permission and we were at an impasse. Then Robbie arrived and things began to move again. We made our second appeal to our Chinese patron: would he write a letter saying we were there as his personal guests? Unhesitatingly he did so and doors began to open. Everyone agreed now that we probably would get permission. It was just a question of when.

There comes a time when a traveller has to make his own fate if he is not to spend forever planning and never doing. One way is to tell enough people that something is going to happen on a certain date so that he will look an idiot if it does not. It is also an effective if risky way of dealing with Chinese prevarication. We announced that whether the permission had come through or not we would leave for Shanhaiguan at the weekend. On the Saturday, as we were signing our contract for our staff and paying the deposit for their wages, we heard that the military had at last agreed a route we could follow all the way from Shanhaiguan to Jiayuguan. We had, of course, asked to be allowed to ride the whole way along the Wall, but we had by now realized that it was most unlikely that permission would be granted for this without restrictions. We knew that of the six provinces we would have to pass through, one – Shanxi – was unlikely to let us travel except by train and that later, in Gansu, the same would apply for some of our route. However, if we could at least make the journey from one end of the Wall to the other and ride for much of the way we would be content. 'Good,' I said. 'I'll come and fetch it.' That, I was told, was quite impossible. The relevant piece of paper was somewhere in the internal security post, which was slow, so that it might take three or four days to emerge. Even then I would not be allowed to see or touch it as it was far too secret. A copy would be given to our interpreter, who would show it to the relevant authorities when necessary. Meanwhile, there was the question of public security. Our Special Travel Permit would not be issued until they too saw the military permission. That would take more time. And time was now running out for us. By now it was 3 May and we had been in Peking over three weeks. Another week's delay would leave us perilously short of time to get to the other end of the wall and home in time for the school holidays which began on 18 July.

'We'll set off for Shanhaiguan tomorrow anyway,' I said, determined not to spend another day in Peking. 'I'll come back and collect the papers when they're ready. At least we can be getting to know our horses and our team while we wait.' Everyone thought we were quite mad and begged us to stay just a few more days until it was all sorted out, but our blood was up and we overrode all objections.

Somehow we did all that had to be done on the last day. The Embassy nurse gave us last minute injections to protect us from Japanese encephalitis. This nasty malady, known in China as boiling brain disease, was transmitted by pigs and several foreigners had recently died from it. Louella rushed around in our gleaming minibus with our crew as soon as they were introduced to us and bought cooking equipment and bedding for them. We had had no choice in our crew's selection, but they looked promising and we would have plenty of time to get to know them better during the next two-and-a-half months.

Our interpreter was Mr Li. Short and always impeccably dressed in a black Mao suit, he had a big round head and a serious, learned manner. In perfect, studied English he introduced himself. 'I, too, am a man of letters,' he said, 'and I also plan to write a book about our experiences. I was a diplomat myself at one time, before becoming an interpreter at your Embassy, and so I know about life.' Although a most unlikely candidate for the rigours we expected, he bravely stood up straight when we asked if he wanted to come, saying he was ready to take part in our 'great exploit'. He reminded us of Mole.

Mr He, our dashing young cook, had won a prize for gourmet Chinese cuisine in Peking. Snappily dressed in a washable safari suit, his dazzling smile assured us that at least one of our party would always be cheerful. He was also a highly qualified Kung Fu artist and he told us laconically that if we were attacked by bandits he could kill three of them with his bare hands and feet before they reached us. Bodyguard, too, it seemed.

The driver was Madam Hao. Round faced and beaming, she was quite the largest woman we saw in China. Her attitude to Louella was one of constant motherly concern. Wrapping her gigantic arms

Madam Hao was quite the largest woman we saw in China. She was very protective towards Louella.

around Louella she would dare the world to molest her charge. We got on well but I suspected she regarded me as something of a brute for subjecting my frail young wife to such a journey. Louella is considerably tougher than I am in most respects but our hosts were all agreed that it was a good thing to have another woman along as otherwise she might be lonely.

And so by Sunday morning we were ready to leave, although still without a single document to show for all the months of planning. Just a letter from our patron 'appreciating the significance' of our forthcoming journey. China is a very strange place. It has changed so very much this century, and yet in some ways it has not changed at all. Things still only get done in the end through the influence of powerful friends and with them almost anything is possible.

3

FINAL PREPARATIONS

On Sunday mornings the Peking Philharmonic perform in the foyer of the Jianguo Hotel, to which we had returned from the Embassy. We felt that Beethoven's Fifth was a good choice for our victorious departure and the friends who came to see us off were impressed, thinking we had arranged it all. Robbie came, of course, with his Californian girlfriend Debra who was in the film business. So too did Mickey Grant. He had appeared at the last moment, having been trying without success to raise financial backing to make a film of our ride. Although it was too late to cover the first part, he and Debra began to discuss the possibility of setting up something for the end.

The Evans family all came after morning service conducted at the Embassy by John Dennis's father, the Bishop of Knaresborough, who was over on a visit. Their presence worked wonders for our status with Mr Li. 'How very gracious of Sir Richard to come in person,' he said.

As we scurried across the foyer carrying our gear from the storeroom to the minibus, our guests drank and shouted at each other over the thundering orchestra. Suddenly we had all kissed each other for the last time, posed for final photographs, squeezed into our overloaded vehicle and we were on our way.

Madam Hao drove very slowly, which was just as well as the only really dangerous thing in China today is the traffic. Foreigners are quite sensibly not allowed to drive outside Peking as the frequency of crashes is almost unbelievable. There are very few cars to be seen and none of them is private, but there are endless overloaded lorries which give no quarter and drive flat out. Thousands of bicycles, even in deep country, vie for the narrow road with uncontrolled carts drawn by horses, mules or donkeys, their drivers often asleep and relying on the draught animal to find its way home. Through these weave noisy convoys of mini tractors pulling vast loads of stones, sand, timber or night-soil. Everyone that has one blows his horn continuously but the road surface is usually so bad and most vehicles rattle so loudly that few can hear anything. We saw three crashes in the first hour, including one where a completely mangled bicycle still lay under a truck. When road accidents occur nothing is moved until the police have completed their investigations. This seems to include leaving the victims in situ as we frequently saw bodies lying among the wreckage. Mr Li told us that the Chinese are reluctant to help anyone after an accident as 'they are still so superstitious that they believe that if they do so they will be responsible for him for the rest of his life'. The nastiest crash of all was much later during the water melon season when a lorry had shed its load after a collision. At first we had thought that there had been no people involved, until we saw broken bodies lying amongst the burst fruit.

A busy main road, such as the one we were following, was like a hellish river of noise, dust and danger flowing through a peaceful countryside where the life of ancient China still continued in its timeless traditional way. The wide expanses of irrigated rice and cornfields were always full of people ploughing behind donkeys or oxen, or pulling ploughs themselves. Hoeing, weeding, planting, rolling, channelling water; there was activity everywhere and when the land was terraced the beauty was overpowering. As though to emphasize the distinction between the two worlds, the roads were lined with mature poplars, so that we could almost imagine ourselves back in France sometimes.

We stopped at midday for lunch at a People's Restaurant. Mr Li threw his weight about, calling for the manager, telling him we were important guests who must have a private room and hygienic food. We were ushered through a big kitchen in which cooks toiled over steaming vats into a dusty courtyard at the back, where we were put in a bare room with one round table and chairs. As we sat down, Mr Li said in his precise English, 'You see, Mr He and I are now going to answer the call of nature. Would you also care to use the loo?' I went with them to a public convenience across the main road. Built of brick, these all followed a standard pattern and were uniformly appalling. Behind a six foot wall were separate enclosures for men and women. The men's consisted of a single open room with four overflowing holes in the ground in a row. The smell was beyond belief and filth was scattered over the floor while the air was thick with flies. Surprisingly, we were to find that this is one of the few areas where foreigners' welfare does not seem to concern the Chinese. There was deep alarm that we would not find comfortable hotels along our route, horror at the prospect of our camping in the countryside, anxiety over our safety and our health, doubt that we could survive on country cooking, but not the least concern that we would have to visit these fetid open sewers each day. Louella assured me that the ladies' was even worse and from then on we did our best to avoid them whenever possible.

Lunch was rather good, as food usually is in China, even in the poorest places, and we all did justice to the dishes of vegetables and meat wrapped in fried dough, sweet and sour pork and omelette which were brought in steaming from the kitchen. During the afternoon we were diverted around Tangshan where, in the terrible earthquake of 24 July 1976, the old town collapsed in a shock registering 8.3 on the Richter scale, one of the biggest ever recorded.

Officially the Chinese say 148,000 people died, but the western estimate was 800,000. We passed the rows of soulless jerry-built highrise apartments which comprise the new city. They already looked shabby and decaying, as though another small tremor would bring them too crashing down.

There were more diversions and delays, so that night was falling by the time we reached the coast at Beidaihe. Since there was still an hour or more to go to Shanhaiguan we decided to spend the night there. Our crew were alarmed at this suggestion, since the idea of spontaneous travel is strange in China, where everything is planned in advance. However, I told them that my guide books named several good hotels and clinched the matter by pointing out that we would certainly be too late for dinner if we struggled on.

Beidaihe is an anachronism. A European seaside resort built in the 1890s by British railway engineers and later taken over by diplomats and businessmen from the capital, it is now being revived as a vacation spot for China's leaders. It is a pretty place, as we found next morning when we had a walk around. There are hills and beaches, solid villas reminiscent of Indian *dak* bungalows set back in pine woods, and a pier. It must have been a lively place in its heyday when there were cabarets and golf clubs. Now it is full of rather determinedly happy Chinese 'working heroes' allowed to escape temporarily from the din of urban life. Mr Li told us that he had started his journal with the words, 'I awoke this morning to the sound of birdsong. This is something I do not hear in Beijing.'

On the beach we found early crowds self-consciously dipping their toes in the cold water and looking as though they felt they should be having fun but were not quite sure what to do. When two boys started wrestling and rolling on the sand, the crowd clapped appreciatively at this manifestation of the holiday spirit. The artificial atmosphere was enhanced by solemn groups of cadres in Mao suits with red badges on their chests, who had clearly earned a break at Beidaihe as a reward for their efforts on behalf of the Party. They strolled together along the shoreline like oyster catchers, with their hands behind their backs, unsure if they approved of what they saw.

A long straight road through acacia and poplar woods on the edge of a wide sandy beach led to Qinhuangdao. In *The Ginger Griffin*, Amber walks these eleven miles and back again, and when she and her companion Burbridge, the ladies' maid, reach Qinhuangdao: '"It puts me in mind of Woking, Miss," said Burbridge; and indeed, except for the prevailing tree being the acacia and not the Scots pine, the residential quarter of Ch'ing-wang-tao [Qinhuangdao] is exactly like the suburbs of Woking.' We saw nothing of the 'commodious, neat and dull' villas she described, but only urban sprawl and factories, which we vowed we would not ride through.

When the time came to try out my own saddle, Tang stood stock still as I settled it on him – and then remained motionless when, in front of a large and interested crowd at the barracks, I mounted and urged him to move. He seemed rooted to the spot and refused to follow Louella and Ming who moved off easily together. Someone brought me a small stick and I struck him gently with it. At once he began a series of jolting bronco bucks, landing hard on all four feet, and accompanied by shrill squeals. I would have had trouble staying on in an ordinary saddle but was quite safe in the deep Camargue one. After a while he settled down and we decided to go for a ride to get the feel of the countryside. This was the big test of whether our whole crazy scheme was going to be even remotely practicable. Out through the barrack gates we went and on to the verge of the main road, Tang skittering nervously at each bicycle. The first lorry to pass us blew its deafening air horn from the moment it saw us until it and its astonished, waving driver were past. This was the pattern followed by almost every other lorry across China, but fortunately the horses paid little or no attention. They were much more interested in the far more numerous donkeys and mules, with whom they were anxious to pass the time of day. I admit to feeling very frightened at this time. It seemed inevitable that something would go badly wrong and for the first time we regretted not bringing hard hats. It had been suggested that we were setting young riders in Britain, who *should* wear hard hats, a bad example by not doing so, but our old Camargue hats were so much more comfortable on a long journey and we would have looked even more ridiculous and strange to the Chinese than we already did. Nonetheless it occurred to me that I would rather look ridiculous on a horse than in a Chinese hospital with a cracked skull. Tang at last stopped bucking, but instead revealed an insatiable desire to kick all other horses, including Ming. This meant I must ride behind or alongside.

With relief we turned left off the main road and were soon in open country. This was more like it. Tracks led off haphazardly and their sandy surfaces were ideal for cantering. We let the horses have their heads and all went smoothly for a while. The brown fields were being cultivated by hand, vegetables planted in neat rows. The people looked up and sometimes smiled, but they never returned our cheerful wave nor responded to our carefully modulated 'Ni hao?' (literally 'You well?', the universal Chinese greeting). The sun beat down on our heads, the horses' hooves threw up dust from the parched earth and far ahead the Wall climbed up into the mountains.

We came to an irrigated area of apple and pear orchards, where pink and white blossom covered the trees. A clear, unpolluted stream ran through, the first we had seen in China, since those near roads and railway lines were always full of litter. Startlingly green lush grass grew beside it and we offered the horses food and drink, but they accepted neither. Everything around us was beautiful and our hearts were bursting with the peculiar happiness which comes when a dream is about to be fulfilled. At last we were doing what we had come to China to do and which everyone had said would be impossible. True, we still did not have our tiresome piece of paper, which might yet be withheld and without which we could not leave, but how marvellous that all our plans, which had been conceived in the ignorance of desperation and necessity, really seemed to work! Only now, as we spontaneously reached out to hold hands as we rode along and revelled in the moment, could we admit how unlikely it was that so many things should have turned out all right. We were going to do it, nothing was going to stop us and it looked as though it would be great fun.

In the distance we saw a small cloud of dust and began to hear a faint approaching rumble. Thinking no evil we watched as we rode, imagining it to be a small lorry being driven fast across country. Suddenly it was on us and we saw that it was a little stallion donkey at full gallop, towing a large iron cart loaded with great rocks which were bouncing out onto the fields. Careering straight at us it began to squeal with excitement. There was little we could do to escape this mad rush except to separate, when it became clear that the object of its intentions, which were manifestly amorous, was Ming. Wheeling around sharply so that the remaining stones were tipped off the cart, it attempted to mount Ming while Louella bravely struck at it with her stick and shouted, 'Shoo!' Fortunately its owner arrived, very out of breath but with enough strength to chase donkey and cart around Louella and Ming a couple of times before catching it and administering a severe beating. He did not seem very pleased with us either, although we could hardly be blamed for the trail of boulders he was going to have to spend the rest of the day gathering up. We rode off: in China the foreigner is generally in the wrong and it was better not to have an altercation about it. We only hoped that Ming did not prove to have the same irresistible attraction for every male donkey in China.

Heading west past Shanhaiguan we crossed the route we had taken on our walk along the Wall and passed through a break in the ramparts. Here we had a most unexpected meeting with a middle-aged Chinese tourist. Incongruous among the toiling peasants, he wore shorts and had a camera around his neck. His reaction to seeing us was quite different to the blank stares of amazement we had already become used to. He had come to see the Great Wall and all its attractions. Clearly we were to be numbered among them and that meant a photograph. Politely but firmly he indicated that we should pose for him against the Wall. It was one of the rare occasions when we could have handed someone our camera and had a picture taken by a competent photographer, but by the time we had thought of it he had thanked us politely and trotted off, carrying the first of our explanatory handouts to be given away. On our French ride we had found that it was invaluable to be able to give those we met a small leaflet explaining who we were and what we were doing, rather than have to explain each time in our fractured French. How much harder to do so in Chinese! Mr Hou and I had concocted suitable wording during my November visit and a kind friend at the Chinese section of the British Museum had written it out in fine characters. With accompanying photographs of us riding the French horses, this had been photocopied 1,000 times and we planned always to carry a stock in our saddlebags. They were invaluable. Roughly translated they read as follows:

English Author and Explorer
Happy Guest Han and Love Baby Lou, husband and wife, are travelling on horses the whole of the Great Wall from Shanhaiguan to Jiayuguan. The Han Lo Bins, approved by the relevant Chinese authorities, are researching and exploring the whole Great Wall from Shanhaiguan to Jiayuguan. Please, all the relevant units and people along this route, give them help and support.

With the Han Lo Bins are an interpreter, cook and driver. We have plenty of food and drink, and a truck and tent.

My Chinese companions may answer all your questions. Thank you.

Soon afterwards we passed a factory. Like many Chinese factories it was stuck out in the middle of the landscape, its chimneys providing a landmark but with few houses around it. As we rode past the air was polluted not only by the smoke and dust but also by a dreadful din from loudspeakers placed at high points around the walls. Beyond we came again to a beautiful watered zone where the aqueducts and streams, which we forded, gave sustenance to tall poplars so that for the first time we rode in the shade. We reached a low ridge and gazed eagerly west along our hoped-for route. It all looked possible and wonderful. We rode back to the town and entered by the North Gate. It was an extraordinary, medieval feeling to ride into an old walled town through a narrow dark gateway. It was made all the more enjoyable by the fact that almost all the other traffic was also four legged and no one regarded what we were doing as the least bit remarkable. The fact that we were European was cause for astonishment, but the fact that we were riding was not.

We called in at the hotel, riding into the courtyard and waking up our surprised crew from their siesta, and then out through the First Gate and into the little extramural village. There we greeted our friend

On Tang and Ming outside Lin Biao's house in Shanhaiguan. Now it is an hotel and we stayed there for a week before setting off.

the muffin man and so went back to the barracks, well pleased with life. The saddles had not rubbed and in spite of having been ridden quite hard for three hours, our horses were not tired and barely sweating. In order to occupy our crew and test some of our equipment we decided to put up our tent. This we did behind the stables, watched by a fascinated crowd of soldiers, with their wives and children. It was a splendid tent, more suitable for a European campsite than for the wilds of China, but since we were not going to have to carry it we had decided to be comfortable. The two sleeping compartments at the sides had built-in mosquito nets and the centre portion was just big enough for the round table and five chairs we had bought in the Friendship Store in Peking before leaving. When Louella and Mr He had sorted out all the kitchen equipment and found nothing vital missing we felt we could, if necessary, be completely independent.

Meanwhile, there was our final problem. Although we had gone ahead over all objections, blithely assuring everyone that all would be well, we still had no guarantee that we would be allowed to set off. I was more worried than I dared admit as, because our time was restricted, a serious delay at this stage would make the whole project unviable and we might have to cut our losses and go home. We both knew how adept the Chinese were at creating delays which could be indefinite. We had, of course, heard nothing from Peking in spite of several faint telephone contacts by Mr Li, each connection taking several hours to come through. We decided that the time had come for him and me to return to Peking and fight the final bureaucratic battle, leaving Louella in Shanhaiguan with Madam Hao and Mr He. Since neither of them spoke a word of English this would be a good chance for her to practise her Chinese, which was improving rapidly.

The train left just before midnight. It had proved impossible to buy soft tickets for Peking but we were reluctantly allowed to try our luck with the train crew on arrival. To our dismay there quite clearly was no space at all on the train when it arrived. We argued and begged at the soft sleepers, hard sleepers and even the hard seats, but we were firmly prevented from getting on. This presented us with a problem as there were no taxis and we had too much luggage to carry back across town to the hotel. To make space in the minibus we were taking surplus equipment back to the Jianguo storeroom, including the two army saddles which had come with the horses and which we now knew we would not need. These we hoped to sell with the horses at the end of the first stage.

'Anyway,' said Mr Li, 'we cannot contemplate awakening them at this hour. We will just have to seek our destiny with the railway system.' The huge station concourse was, as all Chinese stations seem to be at all hours, crowded to capacity with travellers looking as though they were refugees from some disaster. Mr Li seemed quite prepared to join them and let his oriental fate work itself out. Although quite relaxed about the whole matter, as I had my Mozart and a good book with which I could cut myself off from grim reality, I also realized that we might well spend the whole night trying each train that came through without success. As midnight passed it also became my fiftieth birthday. I suggested he track down whoever was in charge and point out that this was all a rather poor advertisement for China. He assured me he would do his best to 'charm the birds out of the trees'. Suddenly everyone became terrifically friendly and we were whisked off behind the scenes to the station master's bare room where I was sat on a chair and given a glass of hot water. The stationmaster was a woman with a striking resemblance to a cross bullfrog, but with a sweet smile which she could unexpectedly bestow on those who, like me, miraculously found favour with her. She escorted us to the 1.30 a.m. train herself and, overriding the protestations of the train director, forced her way into one of the sleeping compartments, which did indeed prove to have only two surprised and sleepy occupants. We were bundled and pushed into the top bunks and she departed telling everyone, so Mr Li informed me, that it was done for the honour of the People's Republic.

At 5 a.m. we were woken by a loudspeaker next to my ear bursting into rousing music at full volume. This time there was no control knob to turn down and we were subjected to such numbers as 'Seagulls over Sorrento' and 'Here Comes the Bride' played at full speed on an electric organ. The current pop music hit, heard all over China on public address systems at this time, was 'Auld Lang Syne' sung in Chinese and we had several renderings of that, too. At the same time there were repeated knockings on our door by the sleeping-car staff trying to make us get up. We all ignored them until 5.45 a.m. when we were made to get dressed and let them make our beds, after which we sat in a row, the others all smoking hard, until we arrived at 8 a.m. Such things are not to be complained of in China. It was enough that my mild criticism of the system and Mr Li's efforts had wrought such miracles in the night.

Then followed one of the most depressing and anxious days I can remember. As it was my birthday I felt I should have been celebrating and enjoying life. Instead I found that nothing had happened and no-one seemed inclined to think that it might. Even worse, my return to Peking instantly confirmed everyone's doubts about whether we would ever get off and I suddenly felt myself shunned like a leper. The cheerful remarks by friends and acquaintances at the Embassy where I went to see if there were any letters (there were none) cut like knives: 'Oh hello, you still here?' 'Well, that's China.' 'I thought it wouldn't be that easy.'

I suddenly seemed to have no friends and spent a maudlin evening contemplating mortality and man's incompetence. Sitting alone in the incredible atrium of the Great Wall Hotel, where I had gone to see if Robbie was in town (he wasn't), I watched the external lifts decorated with fairy lights whizzing up and down between the floors like science fiction rockets. It would be hard to find a greater contrast in the man-made world with the unchanging Chinese countryside, where we had ridden the previous day watching peasants manhandling wooden ploughs. Why is it, I wondered, that when two extremes of man's attainments on earth – tried and tested farming methods and ultimate sybaritic technology – appear to work so efficiently must almost everything inbetween be in such a mess? It was time to go to bed.

The next day I went to see one of our most helpful friends in CITIC, who had patiently spent hours on our behalf finding ways around our problems. I confessed to being in despair that we would never leave. Quietly he quoted to me from the great Chinese classic, by Cao Xueqin, China's Tolstoy, *The Dream of the Red Chamber*: 'The extreme of adversity is the beginning of prosperity.' It is a very Chinese sentiment, but I was grateful for his moral support. An hour later I was told that our military permit had arrived and I could take it to Public Security. There more forms were required, and whilst filling them in I took pleasure from being able to put 'horse' under 'Method of Travel'. They had not had one of those before, but passed it and I was handed the first ever Aliens' Travel Permit starting at Shanhaiguan and ending at Jiayuguan. Although the permitted route was not what we had requested by a long way, it did take us from one end of the Wall to the other and for about half the way we were to be allowed to ride along it. For the first 400 miles west of Shanhaiguan through Hebei and Beijing provinces we were given leave to follow the Wall virtually as closely as we could. Only in the province of Shanxi would we not be permitted to ride at all for 'security' reasons. A long detour by rail and road via Xian was indicated. In northern Shaanxi we were to be allowed to start again on fresh horses and cross the whole of Ningxia. In Gansu we would once again have to go through the 'Hexi Corridor' by train but then we could ride again for the last stretch.

We hurried back to Shanhaiguan to find that Louella had been busy. She had visited Meng Jiang's temple, walked along the beach at the Old Dragon Head and had driven up into the hills to go in a boat on the beautiful Yansai Reservoir. She had even walked back up the Wall along the route we had taken on our first visit, to find that it was being rebuilt. After only two days an astonishing amount had been achieved, and it was being done in exactly the same way as the original Wall had been built. Hundreds of men, each carrying two of the large building bricks, staggered in single file up the slope to deposit their load and return for two more. The mountains are so steep that there would be no other way of doing it. No horse or cart can approach anywhere near most of it and that, of course, is also why we would not be riding on, or even beside, the Wall itself for any of the first stage.

It is very unlikely that anybody ever has or ever will travel the whole way along the Wall itself from one end to the other. Apart from the physical impossibility of anyone except a mountaineer doing so today because of the cliffs which intercept it and its broken condition, the steepness of the terrain through which it passes for the first few hundred miles makes it extremely difficult to stay close to the Wall. Often it runs along a ridge with a sheer drop on either side.

On the other hand travelling close to the Wall, keeping it in sight, would not present any great difficulty even for foreigners, were it not for the man-made problems. In the past these came from the dangers posed by bandits and warlords as well as the natural Chinese suspicion of all barbarians. Today only the latter obstacle remains and that is slowly crumbling.

William Edgar Geil, the only foreigner to have travelled from one end of the Wall to the other before we were granted permission to do so, wrote an infuriating book about his journey*, which became a classic. It is full of Yankee humour but devoid of dates, maps or many details useful to subsequent travellers. There seems little doubt that he did make the journey and there are fascinating photographs of remote sections of the Wall, but there are also huge gaps in the narrative. He describes his 'caravan of mountain mules' travelling on steep ascents in search of the point at which the Wall divides into the Interior and Exterior Walls, stretches from which we were banned as they lie mostly in Shanxi Province; but he also mentions passing Zunhua, a town in the plain below the mountains.

His enthusiasm for the Wall was, however, beyond question. He described it as 'the greatest wall in the world', 'a wall across half a continent', in building which the Emperor Qin, who ruled from 221 to 210 BC, had marked the limits of his empire instead of expanding further. Geil, unusually, saw the Wall as standing for peace, Qin having 'defined a clear and explicit Monroe doctrine for eastern Asia'. He also recognized it as a 'wall of blood', since the Emperor conscripted 300,000 soldiers and 500,000 civilians in one year's mobilization alone. Later emperors condemned even more men to the unbearably hard labour from which often only half survived; nearly two million under the Northern Qi in AD 550, one million under the Sui in AD 607 and many more under the Ming reconstruction and extension of the Wall which went on throughout that dynasty (1368–1644). In some places a death for every metre of Wall was recorded. Not for nothing has it been called the longest graveyard in the world. But on the whole Geil, who must have also suffered frustrating delays before setting out in 1908, a time when the final Imperial dynasty, the Qing, was in its death throes, seems to have admired the achievements of Qin, the builder:

The obstructive mulishness of recent Chinese officialdom presents a strong contrast to the progressive policy of our hero, from which it may be seen that China in the past two thousand years has gone back in the path of progress, or, in other words, has backed the future and fronted the past. Chin, [Wade-Giles spelling of Qin] who possessed immense originality, perhaps went too far in his forward movement, but at any rate there is, and has been for the past two millenniums, an inborn antipathy, a natural resilience on the part of the Chinese from the liberalism of the masterful man from whom China is named by Europeans, but not by themselves.

Until the recent spate of coffee table books on the Great Wall the definitive source of information was Jonathan Fryer's book, published in 1975†. He describes Geil's book as 'the classic description of the

* The Great Wall of China by William Edgar Geil, John Murray, 1909
† The Great Wall of China by Jonathan Fryer, New English Library, 1975

Wall as it was and presumably still is, though nobody has been allowed to retrace Geil's steps since the People's Revolution.'

Later in his book Fryer says, 'Only a handful of other men ever attempted to make significant journeys along the Great Wall, but none ever equalled that of Geil . . . Nobody has ever seen the whole length of the Wall, and no two authoritative maps agree as to its exact course.'

In the introduction he says, 'At the time of writing it seems highly unlikely that any Westerner (or Chinese, for that matter) will have the chance of making a journey along the Wall.' Times had changed and as we lay in Lin Biao's bed on our last night in Shanhaiguan and tried to sleep, we could hardly believe that we were about to prove him wrong.

4

OFF ALONG THE WALL

Ready to leave early, we woke to the sound of heavy rain. It was 10 May and we had been in China for exactly four weeks. During that time we had not seen a drop of rain, which we would have welcomed as relief from the heat and to lay the dust. Coincidentally a two-month drought had broken on the day we had set out on our French ride, unexpectedly soaking us. Now it looked as though we would have to postpone our departure yet another day so as not to start with all our gear wet and a demoralized crew. It was a depressing dawn not helped by Mr Li who said he had been unable to sleep from worrying about our problems. He had had unsatisfactory discussions for hours in the evening with the local authorities who had given him a hard time about our route and our plan to camp along it. All these problems would have been easy to discuss if we could have simply ridden blithely off, but cooped up in the hotel they loomed large and depressed us.

Mr Li was becoming quite neurotic about our prospects and showed signs of losing confidence in our ability to succeed. The impression created by our send off by the British Ambassador was beginning to fade and his morale needed boosting, I felt. A young photographer from Reuters, James King, had been sent out from Peking to cover our departure and this helped to raise our status. 'The pictures he takes of us will be flashed all round the world,' I told Li. 'You will all be famous.' He brightened visibly. James had also brought a recent airmail copy of *The Times* in which my birthday was announced and this impressed Mr Li, restoring our credibility for a time.

At 9 a.m., although it was still pouring down, we decided that it was better to get wet than to go on talking. We went up to the barracks and groomed the horses until their coats shone in the darkness of their smelly stable, while we waited for the rain to let up enough for us to leave. We settled our final accounts with the People's Army, gave the two loyal soldiers a Cathay Pacific T-shirt each and dressed in our full wet weather gear. This consisted of waterproof overtrousers over our leather chaps, and large army capes worn over the top, which spread out to cover the saddles.

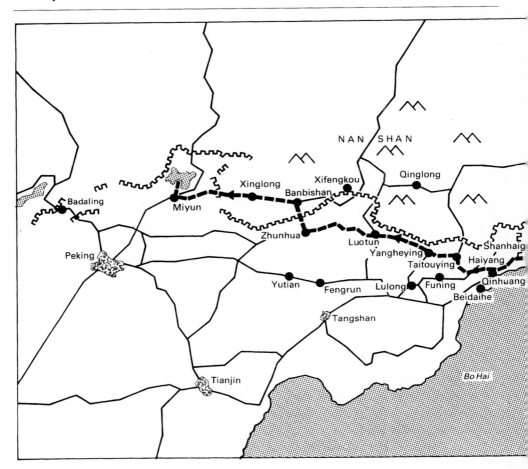

The eastern end of the Wall.

At 11 a.m. it looked a bit lighter and there was even a patch of blue visible in the sky. We saddled up and mounted. Tang took off across the parade ground like a bucking bronco, squealing like a pig, arching his back like a frightened cat and giving a series of abrupt and very uncomfortable bunny hops. I had no trouble clinging on, thanks to my deep saddle, but it was thoroughly unnerving on top of everything else. When he calmed down we rode to the First Pass, where a reception committee from the Antiquities Department and the Shanhaiguan Great Wall Restoration Fund were waiting for us. They pressed us to dismount and take some food and drink with them in their offices, but we declined, saying we really had a very long way to go and must be off. James duly took his pictures of us looking pretty miserable and wet. These were published quite widely in a number of countries, including in *The Times*.

Not knowing how late we would be starting, if at all, we had been unable to fix a rendezvous for the next night with our crew. Chinese maps, if they can be found, are small scale and hard to follow. Madam Hao had one which showed only the major roads. We had brought with us the US Airforce Operational Navigation Charts for the whole of the Great Wall. At a scale of 1:1,000,000 this covered six huge sheets from which I had cut the relevant sections and put them in protective plastic holders. They showed small country roads and tracks as well as many relief features, rivers and much of the Wall itself. The first town marked on our route was Yuguan, but this was a full day's ride away and we would never reach it now. Since we were determined to cut across country along the foothills of the Yan mountains rather than follow the dreadful noisy main road along which we had driven from Qinhuangdao, we didn't know how we would ever meet our crew again. Madam Hao had driven a short way inland on the rough tracks and now resolutely refused to take her minibus that way. We could see ourselves getting lost in the rain, spending a thoroughly unpleasant first night and getting the whole thing off to a bad start. We had left our walkie-talkies in Peking, as permission to use them had not yet been granted and we did not want to risk breaking the law more than necessary. At that moment one of the blue-suited cadres seeing us off suggested a place called Haiyang, which he said was 12½ miles (20 kilometres) this side of Yuguan and on the main road. We promptly agreed to meet there between 4 and 5 p.m., I made a short speech, translated by Mr Li, saying we would accept their kind offer of hospitality when we had done something to deserve it, we waved goodbye and rode off through the town. Once out through the North Gate we felt at last that we were really on our way.

James wanted to take some pictures of us actually on top of the Wall with it disappearing into the distance behind us. We scrambled up, dragging the horses over a place where the Wall had crumbled away, and posed for him on the narrow rampart. It was still drizzling and the visibility was poor. Also the sheer drop on each side made both Tang and me nervous and I was much too frightened to get on him in case he stepped off the edge. Louella and Ming were fearless and so we stood beside them.

Our entourage was still with us when we headed off to the west, leaving the Wall climbing up into the hills on our right. At the village beside the noisy factory we asked for cross country directions to Haiyang only to be told by everyone that we had to go round by the main road as there was a reservoir in the way. Fortunately Louella had been there and so was able to insist that there was a way past below the dam. Reluctantly this was agreed, but we were told we should be sure to lose our way. Realizing this was likely until we became more experienced at finding our way around rural China, I held up a 5 yuan note, offering it as a reward to anyone who would show us the way. An old man on a bicycle pedalled up at that moment and, before he had time to protest, the crowd decided he should be our guide. He was sent off ahead of us looking rather cross and we followed at a canter. It was a good and happy way for us to travel, riding over ideal sandy ground. On the flat our guide was able to outpace us but when we came to hills and he had to dismount we easily caught him up. Chinese bicycles don't have gears. Through pleasant orchards and narrow village lanes we followed, greeting everyone exuberantly in our happiness to be under way and occasionally receiving dazzling smiles in return.

When we reached the wide shallow river bed below the Yansai dam, our cyclist crossed gingerly on stepping stones, wheeling his bike through the water beside him. We splashed through with no trouble. The mountains upstream to our right were magnificent with trees covering their lower slopes and high bare cliffs rising above. They reminded us of the Scottish Highlands. We had given our guide one of our handouts and had seen him stop to read it. When he left us he pointed ahead with a grin saying 'That way to Jiayuguan' which showed a nice and unexpected sense of humour.

We carried on through a succession of small villages where it was easy to imagine we were in the Middle Ages. Pigs outnumbered people, and almost everything was made of wood, clay or straw. The uniform houses had tiled roofs and white paper stuck over the glassless windows to keep the wind out. With summer coming, holes were poked through the paper in places to let the fresh air in, giving the houses a ragged look. Many had old entrance gates with a decorated arch on the top like a church lych-gate. Dogs were still conspicuous by their absence, but there were masses of chickens and ducks as well as small children playing outside their houses. Each had a little garden, sometimes fenced with bamboo or rush palings and often there was a courtyard between the house and the gate. There might be a stable for a mule or donkey and of course an enclosure for the pigs. When these were transported, they were trussed up like chickens and lay quietly on their backs in little carts, wheelbarrows or even across the back of bicycles. Only when their fetters were removed would a deafening squealing begin.

It seemed little effort had been expended to make the houses or gardens pretty. Sometimes there were a few flowers or a painted section of wall but usually everything had an almost self-conscious appearance of squalor and decay. We could never decide whether this arose from a fear of risking standing out from their neighbours in any way, or whether it was simply because China is, after all, still a very poor country and there is no time for such niceties. Here everyone seemed cheerful and well fed. There were no signs of real poverty and the system appeared to be working.

In the villages near Haiyang, each house had a fenced garden where vegetables were grown.

We managed to keep away from the main road until only about an hour out of Haiyang, when we followed the verge safely beside the traffic to a delighted welcome from our waiting crew. Mr Li, looking important in his clean white shirt, black trousers and brown patent shoes, with his black briefcase with its secret documents tucked as always under his arm, barked 'Get down please!' as we rode up.

They were very pleased with themselves at having fixed us up with a stable in a flour mill right beside the road. It was a pretty scruffy and unhygienic flour mill, we thought, just an open courtyard with rubbish everywhere and a huge heap of bones in the middle. They had been dumped there by the butcher next door, who lacked space. A crowd of about sixty people gathered to watch us untack and tie the horses up for the night beside some convenient mangers. There we fed them the rations they had been receiving back at the barracks: 5 pounds (2½ kilos) of maize mixed with 3 pounds (1½ kilos) of bran each per day. We had bought sacks of maize and bran to carry with us in the minibus. Hay or chopped straw for them to munch through the night we hoped to buy at each stopping place and, as it turned out, with all the beasts of burden kept in China, this was seldom a problem.

That night, what with the rain and the late start, we thought it easier to go to a hotel again and we returned to the comfortable one we had been in at Beidaihe a week earlier. But we made it clear to our crew that this was no pleasure trip and there would be no more such luxurious evenings. It was time for Mr He to start earning his keep as cook and for us to start using our camping gear. We had not come to China to stay in hotels.

There are almost no road signs in China and our crew had an aversion to asking the way. Approaching policemen might, I could see, raise all sorts of difficult questions since we were such an unusual party, but it annoyed us that they would almost never stop at intersections and consult the locals. As a result we were constantly getting lost in the minibus. Anyone not familiar with the devious ways through a town, where arbitrary diversions for road works would often peter out in muddy tracks, needed a powerful sense of direction to survive. This Madam Hao patently lacked so that we often had to try and be patient as time, which should have been spent riding in the country, was wasted in dreary suburbs. She managed to get lost leaving Beidaihe, but we passed a wonderfully evocative scene as we drove along the beach. Through the morning mist we could see a row of junks moored off shore. In the still water lines of fishermen, immersed up to their necks at times, carried nets in wide circles out and back to the beach before pulling in great draughts of fishes. It could have been the Sea of Galilee and we half expected to see a white robed figure addressing the multitude.

Once again on mounting I gave the crowd its money's worth as Tang took off across the yard, scattering the heap of bones and departing through the gate in a series of bucks before calming down and behaving well for the rest of the day. We covered the 12½ miles (20 kilometres) to Yuguan in under 2½ hours, a good average speed of about 5 miles (8 kilometres) per hour. With occasional canters but mostly walking, this was about the best we could expect the horses to maintain for a whole day.

At Yuguan Mr Li had made enquiries and found that there was a track through the mountains to our next night's proposed stop at Yangheying. It was too rough for the minibus, which would follow the main road via Funing to meet us in the evening.

We now turned in to riding country which we felt at the time was unlikely to be improved upon for beauty and perfection in China. A charming earthen country lane led between an avenue of poplars beside a stream bed towards dramatic mountains where we could spot occasional watch towers of the Wall. As the land rose there were areas of terracing interspersed with open plains where we could let the horses have their heads and canter to the horizon. Birds were everywhere and their singing in the trees filled the air. Swallows, swooping low after the rain, almost passed between the horses' feet. Ordinary house sparrows chirped noisily but were outdone by bulbuls and babblers. I wished I were better at identifying them. There were yellow warblers which sang very sweetly and a small black and white

Usually our cheerful greetings were ignored as we rode past, but sometimes the ice was broken and we received friendly smiles.

woodpecker with a bright red flash underneath. Surprisingly, too, the birds seemed tame, as normally in China they are harried. In the fifties there was a crazy policy to try to wipe out sparrows on the principle that they competed with man for food. They were classified as one of the 'Four Pests' with rats, flies and mosquitoes. Of course, wherever this was tried, there was an immediate explosion of the crop pests and insects normally eaten by the birds. During the Great Leap Forward in 1958 there was even a theory that if the peasants cut down all the trees around their villages they could make fertilizer by burning them and spreading the ashes on their fields. As a result they had no fuel for cooking and heating and that policy has been reversed in recent years with a vengeance. Now it is compulsory for everyone to plant trees and the evidence is everywhere. Wherever there was steep, barren or otherwise unusable land near villages we saw plantations of conifers, and rows of poplars lined even the most humble tracks.

Back from the track there were apple orchards with more trees planted as shelter belts. It was a hazy day but not too hot and everywhere there were people working in the fields. Nearly all the work was being done by hand and we learned how to recognize from people's gait what jobs they were doing. A woman planting seed moved in a curious 'dot and carry one' way as she dropped each seed and then stamped it into the ground. A man using his weight like a roller walked slowly with tiny rapid steps, shuffling his feet along to compress the soil. Others piled earth or manure into small heaps all over their plots, to be spread later. Sometimes we saw larger, older mounds among those dotting a field and realized they were graves. These might have some paper stuck on the top or a few stones, occasionally even a tombstone, but they seemed to be placed entirely at random and were ploughed right around.

At the head of the valley we came to a larger, rather pretty village where a stone bridge spanned the stream. Next to it was tethered an unexpectedly fine bay stallion, which whinnied and tried to escape and join us. Here we turned left up into the foothills of the mountains through a narrow gorge between big black basalt rocks and towering outcrops above. On a grassy slope with a few young trees beside a clear pool in the stream where there were fishes we stopped and unsaddled the horses for their midday rest. They grazed greedily while we lay and nibbled sweet biscuits and raisins, holding the ends of their neck ropes. It was an idyllic spot. A small, pregnant donkey was tethered across the stream. To our relief it took no interest in Ming and ignored us all. The sun shone and a breeze kept the air cool while drying the sweat on the horses' backs and their saddle cloths. Overhead a pair of red-billed choughs wheeled and turned, their familiar trilling churrs carrying clearly to us. The chough is the emblem of Cornwall, where we live, and they were once very common there, but are now extinct in the wild. I have long been involved in various schemes to reintroduce them to the county after which they are often called Cornish Choughs and I have watched flocks of them performing their aerobatic displays in different parts of the world. I knew that they were to be found right across Asia but I had not expected to see them so soon. As these two flew down to us and called to each other before disappearing up the valley, they were like a signal that all would be well on our journey.

An old grey-bearded man walked slowly up the track from the village and stopped to pass the time of day. 'Women shi Yingguo ren ['We are English'],' we said, and he nodded gravely, repeating 'Ying-guo ren' as though he met English people every day. 'Women yao chu Taitouying ['We want to go to Taitouying']' we tried, and he calmly pointed ahead up the hill, the way we were going. 'Women chi ma Chang Cheng ['We are riding horses along the Great Wall'],' we told him, and he looked doubtful, so we gave him one of our leaflets to prove it, and he strolled off reading.

We felt inordinately pleased with ourselves at having been able to discuss where we were from, where we were going and what we were doing without any help. For the first time we were able to take a deep breath and realize that, if nothing else went right, we would have experienced the pleasure of being independent in China, which was our real quest. We were fascinated by the Wall and eager to see as much of it as possible, but it was really what Freya Stark calls 'a thread to run one's exploring on', which enabled us to be in places as intriguing and remote as this one.

As we mounted and rode on, we found that it was indeed well worth all the effort that had gone into getting us here. To our left two steep boulder-strewn mountains had groves of stunted pines and willows nestling in their valleys. On our right a sheer rock, black on the outside, red where flakes had fallen away, stood up a thousand feet, bare of all vegetation save for a few tufts of grass and scrub clinging to the crevices. We were in a classical Chinese landscape and the scenery on each side could have been painted on long hanging watercolour scrolls. The road ahead climbed up into the hills in a series of hairpin bends between which we could dismount and lead the horses up steep short cuts while the cart track followed the contours. In one of my favourite childhood books, *The Box of Delights* by John Masefield, the old magician Cole rides into just such a picture hanging on the study wall in order to escape from his enemies. We too felt capable of anything at that moment, as though the whole of the long journey ahead, which we were now confident of completing, could be grasped and enjoyed in one charmed moment. I have always found on expeditions that for every one good moment such as this there are nine bad ones when worry or discomfort predominate. The extraordinary thing about our long rides together has been that both Louella and I have found the proportions happily reversed so that nine tenths of our travel time has been supremely enjoyable. I do not believe that anyone can honestly say the same of driving, walking, sailing, climbing, running, flying or any other means of travel.

From the top we had a splendid view back through the gorge. On the far side tightly terraced slopes led down to a fertile valley far below, which it took us another hour to reach. As we crossed a river on the edge of the village of Taitouying, a proud pair of Chinese geese swam under the bridge below us. A flock of sheep kept their heads down in the afternoon sun, huddled in a tight circle trying to share a minute patch of shade. A big watch tower on a peak marked the Wall and once again we turned left to ride west and parallel with it. The landscape continued to surprise and delight us with its unspoilt beauty. Most of the time we were on a pleasant sandy track running through wild rocky country beside a stream. Whenever we passed through villages it became muddy and narrow; life there must be pretty unpleasant in the winter when it is very cold and often wet. We were probably passing at the ideal time, before the heat and dust became too great, while the blossom was still out on the fruit trees and patches of grass and wild flowers carpeted the hillsides.

By 6 p.m. we were all getting fairly tired and anxious to arrive. We had been on the road for nine hours and calculated that we must have covered 40 miles (62 kilometres). Our crew had found somewhere for the horses, but had bad news and long faces about our own accommodation. The local authorities had been adamant that we could not stay in Yangheying ourselves as it was a 'security area'. Instead we had to be driven to the county town of Lulong, where there was a hotel. Too tired to argue much, we saw the horses fed and settled for the night and allowed ourselves to be led through the dark by an army jeep. Poor Mr Li was almost in tears from the constant arguments he had been having on our behalf. Although we had technical permission to be where we were, the whole concept of what we were doing was so new and alarming that no one was prepared to take the responsibility for letting us camp or stay in remote villages. Kindly but firmly, they insisted that the only hotel suitable for foreigners was in Lulong and so that was where we must go, however time consuming and expensive that might be for us. Deciding to make the best of it we asked on arrival if they had hot water, as a bath is especially welcome after a long day in the saddle. 'Oh yes, of course,' they said, and Louella gave Mr Li a hug and told him it was all for the best.

The hotel was a grim compound with rooms leading off, a familiar design in China for anything from factories to hotels to abattoirs. Mr He was given a room to cook in and we lit his kerosene stoves for the first time. Mr Li, his sleeves rolled up as he scraped the scales off a large fish, said kindly, 'Too many cooks spoil the broth! You go and have a hot bath.' We did not argue. There was, however, no water in the taps and when we asked about this back in the kitchen we were told, 'Oh yes, there is hot water in the thermos flask for making tea. None in taps.'

When we were called for supper we found that Mr He had created an incredible feast. With the couple of pounds we had given him to spend in the local market, he had bought a huge flat fish like a turbot, which he had cooked on the bone in oil. He had made another dish of fried fish with straw potatoes and yet one more of sumptuous diced sweet and sour fish pieces. There were two pork dishes – one breaded, one with a delicious garnish – eggs and pancakes, vegetables, and an astonishing fresh fruit salad, each dish better than the last. He served it with panache, too, coming in at the last moment to sprinkle a dash of salt and pepper over the dishes with a flamboyant gesture and then joining us to tuck in with a will. His good humour and energy were infectious and it was impossible to be grumpy in his company. His only failing was that he tended to smoke throughout the meal and to stub his cigarettes out in the empty dishes. It was nearly midnight before we were in bed and we were up again at 5.30 a.m.

As I saddled up Tang I looked under his tail and noticed that he had a nasty open sore just where the crupper of my Camargue saddle went. It must have rubbed him painfully, especially first thing in the morning, and doubtless explained his extraordinary antics. I had described him to Reuters as having 'a severe personality defect' and this had been reported in the press to the amusement of our friends at home. Now I felt really bad at having failed to notice the cause sooner. Without the crupper, which served no useful purpose if we weren't going to do any more rodeo riding, he behaved perfectly and we made a steady 4½ miles (7 kilometres) an hour all day.

Now the Great Wall was visible most of the time on our right, sometimes only a mile or two away. It was exciting to see how much of it was still there. Although totally unrestored and neglected since the end of the Ming dynasty in the sixteenth century it seemed to be virtually intact. Grass and weeds grew between the building blocks and the watch towers and crenellations had crumbled, but it was still a massive and awe-inspiring piece of building. Once we were able to count twenty-seven watch towers on the horizon where a great line of mountains stretched away into the distance. At other times they seemed to ring the plain around. There the Wall came right down to our level before rising up into the hills again and disappearing.

Walls were built to divide warring states and to define borderlines as early as the fifth century BC, but it was not until China was unified by the First Emperor Qin in 221 BC that they were first linked up and extended to form the Great Wall. The Wall we were attempting to follow was mainly the Ming Wall, built between 1403 and 1424, incorporating sections of earlier Walls. This has always been described as being 10,000 li long, a figure denoting great length rather than an exact amount. With a li equalling about a third of a mile (half a kilometre) this would put the Wall at 3,333 miles (5,000 kilometres). In fact if all its extensions are counted, it has been estimated to be 3,930 miles (6325 kilometres) long, but if only the main continuous route between Shanhaiguan and Jiayuguan is counted, then a figure of 1,850 miles (2977 kilometres) is arrived at. This is about exactly the distance from Land's End to John O'Groats and back again. Geil estimated that there had once been as many as 25,000 towers with another 15,000 isolated watch towers along its length. It seems an incredible figure, but in places they are only 100 yards (91 metres) or so apart, although many have now been destroyed, particularly in the western part.

In 1793 Captain Parish, military attaché to Lord Macartney, the first British Ambassador in China, first saw the Great Wall at Gubeikou, further along the stretch which we were now riding beside. He was so impressed by its size that he made the famous calculation, recorded by John Barrow, Macartney's private secretary, that if it was really 1,500 miles long then it would contain as much bulk as all the dwelling houses in England and Scotland together. 'Nor,' he goes on, 'are the projecting towers of stone and brick included in this calcula-

The Wall we were following was mainly the Ming Wall built in the early fifteenth century.

tion. These alone, supposing them to continue throughout at bowshot distance, were calculated to contain as much masonry and brickwork as all London . . .'

Innumerable battles were fought over the centuries in these mountains. Most took place at the passes which guarded the main routes through the Wall leading to the capital. At night the gates were shut and guarded by a thousand men. From the end of the Ming dynasty there were always two officers in charge, one Manchu, one Chinese, to avoid treachery. One of the last great battles at the Wall was commanded by Lin Biao, leading the Communist Red Army during the Sino-Japanese War (1937–45). He ambushed and massacred a Japanese division, using the ruined Wall on either side as cover as they passed through the narrow defile of a pass. Later, after defeating the Nationalists in the crippling civil war which followed the defeat of the Japanese, he was to lead his exhausted but victorious troops south through these mountains, over the Wall and into the heart of China.

As soon as we stopped in a village a crowd would gather from nowhere and we would begin to feel the claustrophobic effect of several hundred pairs of eyes fixed unblinking on us. It was tempting to prevent this happening by cantering through some villages so that we would be gone before anyone noticed how unusual we were. This made us feel like Mongol invaders or Ming nobles hurrying up to defend the Wall and sometimes it seemed that little had changed since those days.

We were determined that we would not be forced again to drive to a hotel but would stay with our horses. In Luotun, which we reached in mid-afternoon to rendezvous with our crew, we told the local official that this was what we intended doing. We had wanted to force our crew to camp with us by simply riding on until we came to a suitable place and then stopping without telling anyone, but this had proved impossible. One reason was that even here, far off the beaten track and on a bumpy country road, there were so many people that the sort of campsite I had in mind simply did not exist when we needed it. Secondly, and more important, as we would have put up with the crowds which would inevitably appear whenever we camped, we came to realize that we simply could not put our crew in such a position. It was not just that they did not much like the idea of camping and regarded any human habitation as vastly preferable. It was the unavoidable fact that they could get into terrible trouble if anything went wrong. They had to inform the local authorities of our presence and our intentions. They in turn had to inform senior authorities and nobody was going to risk the penalties they would have to pay if, as a result of letting us have our way, we had an accident or were robbed. In the event of a serious accident, such as one of us having to go to hospital, for example, we were told quite seriously that the person held

People gathering on the compound wall and the hillside beyond to watch as we put up the tent.

to be responsible might well be executed. Reluctantly we had to accept that this was no exaggeration and we must play it by the book.

For a couple of hours we sat and fumed in the official's bare office, while he tried vainly to contact the next county town on his hand-cranked telephone and the horses waited patiently in the sun outside. Suddenly, without any success or extra persuasion from us, he decided at 6 o'clock that we could camp in his compound. With a burst of energy we set to work. The whole town gathered on the compound wall and the hillside beyond to watch as we put up the tent, blew up our mattresses, laid out our bedding and set up the table and chairs. Mr He needed no encouragement to repeat the previous night's culinary triumph with fresh ingredients and we all had a very merry and public evening. During the night it poured with rain, but we were warm and dry in the tent and we awoke to thick mist. When we looked out through the flap at dawn we could have been at sea and everything was soaked. The horses had spent the night in a shed and were fine, but we thought it better to wait until the tent had dried a bit before helping to pack it up as otherwise it could be ruined.

We pottered about having a leisurely breakfast of coffee and muesli. This was easily made from the packaged material we had with us and the thermos of hot water which was nearly always produced. Our crew worried about finding a proper Chinese breakfast somewhere in town and this helped to get them moving in the mornings. They could never understand how glad we were to forego this pleasure and settle for a biscuit or two instead of enormous quantities of pickles.

At 7.30 a.m. the sun broke through the fog and hit the tent. At once we all sprang into action, took it down and put it away damp. In no time we were off into a glorious sunny day with the clarity that comes after rain. The Wall looked close enough to touch, with little white clouds scudding past the towers. And the countryside, too, was beautiful. It reminded us of Tuscany, seeming highly civilized and well tended. Yesterday had been all brown parched plains with toiling peasants as far as the eye could see. The bare hills were being cultivated right to the top sometimes, with terracing in ever narrower rows until it was hard to believe the output could be worth the effort. It was not just the aftermath of rain which gave today a different feel. The region was undoubtedly richer and the atmosphere more relaxed and prosperous. The fields, many still terraced, but in wide generous swathes, ran only a short way up the hills, which were thereafter thickly wooded with pines and acacias. It was as though the people here could afford to leave the harder land to nature, since she had been generous to them in the lowlands. There, too, were plenty of trees, fine massive poplars along the roads and orchards of ancient gnarled walnuts as well as the usual apples and pears. The soil beneath was a rich red and all the rivers and streams were running, even if sometimes they were only a trickle between grassy green banks.

In the villages the houses were of a better quality and the gardens well tended, with wallflowers and morning glory among the vegetables. Many of the houses had wall paintings on them, well executed and charming. The standard design of house in this part of Hebei is perfect for these paintings, as the end walls have no windows and provide a wide blank space. Here we saw delicate and imaginative pictures of deer, storks, even goldfish. The tiled roofs had curled-up eaves and sometimes there were even models of storks and egrets in pairs on the ridges. In the streams girls in bright colours washing clothes made irresistible pictures.

For four hours we rode through this seeming paradise and everything was good. We had lost the stiffness of the first few days' riding and the horses were going really well. Ming had a delightful habit of breaking straight from walk to canter with a little hop when Louella tapped him gently with her stick. We would then lollop along, side by side, holding hands, leaning back in our armchair saddles and enjoying the sunshine while the horses did all the work. We agreed that if it had been possible we would have liked to take Tang and Ming home with us to Cornwall, where they could be put to good use on the farm, but we knew it could not be.

We gave up making cheery advances to the locals, and chatted happily to each other as people pushing wheelbarrows, wheeling bicycles, driving donkey carts, and working on their crops stared at us in blank amazement. A few were very friendly and called out to us. When we passed a small roadside factory all the men came running out making urgent drinking gestures to us, begging us to stop and join them. But we regretfully explained we had a long way to go, and distributed our handouts.

The road was made of packed earth, smooth and therefore usable by the minibus as well as being perfect for riding on. The acacia trees along it were covered in white flowers and the smell was strong and heady, like orange blossom. We were caught up by our crew at midday where we had unsaddled the horses by a grassy stream so they could drink and graze for an hour. There had been no hay for them at last night's camp. We took out the tent and spread it on some convenient round roadstones to dry. With the hot sun and the rising wind this took only fifteen minutes, after which the crew sped off, anxious to find somewhere they could have a good lunch as breakfast had been disappointing and they were depressed. They reminded me of compilers of gourmet food guides scouring one of the culinary regions of France like Perigord or Tourraine for fine restaurants. This is not so strange, perhaps, in a country where for all the austerity and deprivations, both physical and cultural, of recent history, appreciation of good food has always been acceptable. With the small sum we gave them each day to buy food for themselves and an evening meal for us all they were relatively rich and determined to enjoy it. As for us, we opened a small tin of corned beef and did not envy them. One Chinese meal a day, we found, was quite enough. We were constantly amazed by their capacity for food as were they by our abstinence.

A friendly crowd had gathered to watch us and some had babies with them. It had been our son's first birthday a couple of days before and I was having trouble getting Louella past anything that age. Soon the babies were being passed to her one by one for a quick cuddle. With their split trousers instead of nappies, out of which their little pink bottoms protruded, they were rather endearing but I tended to leave this excellent method of cementing Anglo-Chinese relationships to her.

Cantering off to cheers and waves we immediately ran into very different conditions as the elements began to do the dirty on us. The weather in China is notoriously unpredictable and we were soon being chilled by an icy wind which became rapidly stronger until we were riding with our heads down into the teeth of a gale. Great swirls of dust were whipped up by the wind and carried off across the wide river valley we were passing and high up into the air. We had heard that this was the season of the dust storms which plagued the whole of northern China, including Peking. We soon had grit in our eyes, noses, teeth and

Tang resting after a long day's ride through the Chinese countryside.

inside our clothes. The horses hated it. They played up and tried to turn round or leave the road. Several times we had to ride across low concrete bridges and felt ourselves in danger of being swept off. From here there were wonderful views leading up and down the river valleys, vistas of distant hills past groves of willows and poplars where cattle grazed in water meadows. But we could barely look up for the wind and the dust. All afternoon it continued and we began to ache for it to stop. Each time we rounded a corner or crossed a ridge of hills we told ourselves it would be better but it never was until the evening. I tried to photograph the storm, but found to my intense irritation that the camera was broken. We had two Pentaxes, one loaded with colour, and one with black and white film. For some reason we only had the black and white with us that day and now I found that the film was not winding on; the sprocket was broken. This annoyed me quite unreasonably and I stayed in a foul mood for the rest of the day. The dust storm did not help. I had not met a worse one for more than twenty years when, at an oasis called Bardai, high in the Tibesti Mountains of Chad, I remembered trying to capture on film palm trees bending to the wind, only faintly visible through the driving dust just like the poplars were now.

At Santunying we found our crew cheerful and deservedly pleased with themselves, having erected the tent on a hard piece of ground in the shelter of a wall with quite a pleasant stable nearby for the horses. This was owned by a cheerful and garrulous old lady who produced and sold us 25 pounds of hay and promised to watch over them during the night. While I grumpily fiddled with my camera in the tent, Louella charmed the local population by producing our Polaroid. Mr Li was, I think, rather shocked by the easy way she fraternized with mothers and children, communicating in the universal language of motherhood, helped by her growing command of Chinese words. The initial crowd which had gathered on our arrival never lessened, but as the word spread that Louella was a sucker for babies and could actually produce instant photographs of them, women kept drifting in with their children, noses wiped and woolly hats on straight, hoping.

Many of the people still wore blue Mao suits, but these were mostly the senior officials of the villages, the cadres. Working clothes for men were usually old army fatigues, shapeless overalls in olive green. The very old were almost always dressed in black, the ladies often still in the traditional droopy trousers tied at the ankle and with a black smock over the top. Everyone wore long johns underneath at all times, whatever the temperature. These were usually bright red and often exposed up to the knee because of the peculiar Chinese habit of rolling one trouser leg up. We were never able to work out why they did this, in the boardrooms of Peking as well as the paddy fields of Hebei, but guessed it might be a way of cooling off from the excessive heat of their long underwear.

The women were much more colourful and it was clear that, after decades of austerity and conformity in dress, they were cautiously and inexpertly beginning to let themselves go. While blue and drab green were still the predominant colours, a girl might have a brilliant scarlet cravat. Pink, maroon, purple and lime green were popular for scarves and we saw some outrageous straw hats, as seen at village fêtes in England. Most of the men wore green forage caps of a standard design, which seemed to be regulation garb, but among them sprouted some surprisingly natty check cloth caps. And whilst in the countryside all girls wore trousers and skirts were never seen, some had garish check jackets, the colours in violent mixes such as green and red, puce and brown and even once orange and purple. But these were only rare flashes of colour on the more adventurous adults and it was with the little children that they really went to town. Some had little lace-embroidered bonnets or brightly coloured knitted bobble caps. Many had quilted jackets in silk or cotton, well padded, on which all the pent up exuberance of the parents and grandparents to stitch and embroider had been let loose. White knitted jackets, too, were worn with flower-patterned trews and little purple bootees. The colour combinations were often shattering but the pleasure and love with which these children were dressed was very evident. In fact the official policy of one child per family is creating many problems, with a generation of pampered, over-indulged children growing up who need to be taught at school how to behave and look after themselves. Concerned articles regularly appear in the Chinese press on this topic, where they are referred to as 'little emperors'. The rule is being relaxed in rural areas but it is still strictly enforced in the cities. One problem is that although female infanticide is never mentioned and would be severely punished if detected, a ratio of seventy-five male births to twenty-five female has been recorded in some areas. Most Chinese families would still greatly prefer to have a son.

Another delicious feast from Mr He finished off the evening well. This time he had acquired a chicken and, as with the fish, he had managed somehow to make three dishes from it. Every scrap was used, including the head, which, being a great delicacy, was pressed on Louella. Eggs, too, for which we had expressed a desire, had been found and he produced two amazing omelettes, one with pork and cucumber, one with dried shrimps. While small boys sat in a row watching our every move intently, we went to bed in our tent to read for a while by candlelight, to listen to the BBC World Service news on our small radio and to feel satisfied that it had not been a bad day at all in the end.

When our crew joined us later, the night became less tranquil, since the Chinese share with most Eastern people a doubtless admirable lack of inhibitions about bodily functions. Their three daily square meals inevitably resulted in the build up of gases, which were noisily expelled for the next few hours. Sharing a small tent with so many people was a new experience for Louella. 'We are positively cheek by jowl,' said Mr Li, as he turned in. Fortunately we were both usually tired enough to sleep through anything.

5

THROUGH THE MOUNTAINS

The gale in the night which kept us awake worrying about whether our tent would blow away turned out to be mostly an illusion caused by the loud noise of the wind in the poplars. All morning the Wall was visible on our right again through the sunny air now clear of dust and we went fast along a good wide verge towards the big county town of Zunhua. As we approached, the houses became bigger with more gardens and a general air of prosperity. It was a fertile plain we were riding through and the villages were busy with street markets selling a wide variety of vegetables. Spring onions and bunches of radishes were commonest at this time of year but there were also apples and pears for sale which must have been stored through the winter. We bought some of these to munch as we rode. On butchers' tables great chunks of fatty pork were displayed chopped into shapeless lumps and sold by weight on hand-held scales. The big white buns we had had in Shanhaiguan were on sale, as were yellow loaf-sized cakes, and rings of hard plaited bread. Big pancake fritters were being fried at the roadside. Maize was for sale by the sack or the handful and everywhere we saw girl ice cream vendors on bicycles. They carried a white wooden box mounted behind them and cried their wares in singsong voices which carried a long way. 'Bin guen' they called, which sounds, when shouted, very like Yingwen, meaning English, and we thought for a time they were drawing unnecessary attention to us. At first we were dubious about sampling their wares as they were usually kept cool by being wrapped in damp old sacks which looked none too clean and when unwrapped they appeared to have been made of muddy ditch water. But once we had taken the plunge, tasted how good they were and found that we did not instantly go down with dysentery, there was no reason not to carry on. The cry was to be heard right across China and the ices were a great comfort on hot days. They cost 10 fen or 2p.

Often we found ourselves being escorted by a bevy of bicyclists, who pedalled along beside us gazing curiously at the strange sight we presented. When we bade them good day they would often drop back in confusion to giggle among themselves before speeding up for another look. Then we would give them a handout and they would drop behind again while they stopped to read it. One would read aloud while the others clustered around peering over his shoulders in a scrum. On catching us up again they would ask us where we were going and we could practise our Useful Phrases. We had by now developed a valuable technique with these and we could slip in a couple of simple jokes to show we were human. It was easy to say that we were English, *not* American, which always went down well as there is still a legacy from the days when effigies of Uncle Sam were burned in public as the big bogeyman. Explaining that our horses were good Chinese ones and not English usually brought another laugh, but the most successful ploy was always to apologize profusely for not being able to speak Chinese and then hit them with the acutely embarrassing question as to whether any of them spoke English. This would inevitably produce a chorus of shamefaced denials as, although everyone in China now learns English in school, few in the countryside will dare to try it out without warning and the rehearsal of chosen phrases.

One of our bicycling companions for a time had a huge load of vegetables tied on behind him and draped over the handlebars. When we stopped to buy ice creams from one of the girls, he insisted on paying and then invited us into his house for a drink. Reluctantly we had to refuse as we were aware that there were barely enough hours in the day to cover the 30 miles (50 kilometres) or so we had set ourselves and to delay might mean we would not arrive at our destination before nightfall. But it was extraordinarily kind of him; with average incomes in the countryside recently calculated at below £100 a year, an expenditure of 4p on strangers was generous.

At Zunhua a major market was under way and we wondered if we would be able to get through the town. By the time we thought of trying to find our way round through the suburbs it was too late and we were being swept along in a tide of humanity. There was a solid mass of people as far as we could see in all directions, many pushing loaded bicycles, prams or hand carts piled with produce. Others drove donkeys almost invisible beneath their loads of brushwood. Through this, somehow, incredibly, a certain amount of traffic moved. One or two lorries, like whales in a shoal of fishes, blew their horns constantly and inched forward. We flowed along in their wake. Everyone was cheerful and busy, stopping to haggle at stalls along the sides or in the middle of the road to buy produce straight from the carts. They seemed very pleased as well as astonished to see two Europeans on horses riding through the middle of the bedlam. Fortunately the horses were very good and kicked no one. It also helped, I found, to take lots of photographs as we rode to divert people's attention from the possibility of objecting to our presence. And it was a wonderfully colourful scene we saw over the heads of the crowd. In little tents on

Roadside cobblers proffering on the pavement a while-you-wait service resoling shoes with strips of rubber.

the roadside men were having their heads shaved by barbers and they waved cheerfully at the camera. Cobblers with contraptions that looked like antiquated Singer sewing machines proffered a while-you-wait service resoling and patching. Beside them were pieces of rubber cut into the rough shapes of feet. Spread on the ground or on trestle tables everything under the sun was being sold. Tobacco was on offer by the leaf, bicycle parts, cheap plastic sunglasses, strips of linoleum and all sorts of implements: trowels, shovels, sickles, spades, hoes. Then there were lengths of wire and hemp rope, steel mesh, nuts and bolts and an extraordinary lethal design of rat trap, like a giant homemade mousetrap, which seemed very popular. Among all this was a wide variety of animal life on its way to the livestock section of the market. Sheep and goats were being dragged by ropes and everywhere pigs were tied on to wheelbarrows, carts and bicycles in the most uncomfortable looking way, their squeals drowned by the deafening ambient noise level. Everyone was shouting cheerfully at everyone else and there was no doubt that they were all having a good time.

It took us an hour to force our way through the town and out the other side. As we were swept out into the less congested outskirts surrounded by a merry crowd taking their purchases home, we met what looked like a haystack coming towards us. Somewhere under the

Rush matting being woven on the pavement in front of a photographer's window. Free enterprise at work.

sweet smelling new mown hay was a tiny donkey forging stolidly ahead. On top of the load was a spectacular rose bush in full bloom.

Soon afterwards we reached the mountains and the Wall. We stopped under it for a rest and a picnic beside a wide shallow stream. It ran through a village which had been built from the stones of the Wall, so that there was no gate or proper pass any more at this point. Fortunately our picnic site was a short distance away from the nearest houses and so we had some time to ourselves before the crowds arrived to watch us. We unsaddled the horses and tied them on long ropes to convenient poplars so that they could graze. Ming's saddle had begun to rub him in a few places and although the skin was not broken and he was clearly not troubled by the spots, it was a worry. So, too, was some slight lameness in Tang, who had been favouring his near foreleg. There seemed to be no swelling but we had been pushing the horses hard and they were due for a day of rest.

We washed in the stream, ate some biscuits as well as a small tin of peaches and lay back in the sun to rest, well pleased with life. For a while we slept. I opened my eyes to see above me the face of an old grey-bearded sage looking solemnly down at the two strange barbarians who had materialized in his village. He had a timeless face, which could have looked just so at any travellers in any era. We were just his first Europeans.

Once on the other side of the Wall there was a marked change in the landscape. Because for the last few days we had been seeing from the plain below watch towers and stretches of Wall silhouetted against the sky, we had imagined that it ran along the watershed. But at this point the Wall guarded the southern foothills of the mountains. North of it the road climbed steeply up a series of hairpin bends. Looking back we could see how there was still a square enclosure on the steep slope above, where the great gate must have been. The Wall here was crenellated on both sides, which is unusual as normally only the outer northern face needed defending. Impressive and largely intact, it curved away up the hill and along the ridges to the east and the west. The towers were closely spaced as this must once have been an important place to defend, one of the handful of strategic passes between the Hebei plain and the Mongolian plateau. Through these the Chinese emperors used to cross the Wall on their way to their hunting grounds and their summer residence; the Palace of Chengde was barely fifty miles to the north. They were also among the sections of Wall most likely to come under attack.

The first rule observed by the Wall's builders was to follow the terrain so that signals could be flashed as quickly as possible from one watch tower to another and at the same time be seen far back behind the line of the Wall so that reinforcements could be sent up quickly in the event of an attack. The result is the extraordinarily dramatic appearance of the Wall throughout its length. Incredibly steep ridges are followed along their crests both because they form natural barriers themselves and also because huge boulders and sheer cliffs were used in the building to save on bricks.

The hillsides were thickly wooded with sizeable trees of many varieties, the first proper woods we had seen. Sweet chestnut was mixed with oak, pine, birch and masses of gloriously flowering acacias, their great clusters of white flowers giving off a heady scent. Beside the road in terraced plantations were orchards of all sorts of fruit trees which we could not identify. From the top of the path there was a wonderful view back over the Wall and the plains beyond. Tartar horsemen must have once ridden through the forest to this ridge and looked out at the land they planned to conquer. In a few more yards we came to a much more harsh and rugged prospect. Jagged peaks stretched as far as the eye could see and way below us was a river valley. There, like an oasis in the desert, we could see the green trees of the little town of Banbishan, where we planned to stop and rest for a couple of nights.

Everything was ready for us when we arrived. We were led to a similar courtyard to those we had been using but this one, Mr Li told us, rather craftily we thought, was also a hotel. We could pitch our tent there if we wished but as the ground was very hard and the rooms were

Tartar horsemen must have once ridden through this pass between Zunhua and Banbishan.

only 60p a night, why not use them? We knew he and the others thought us quite mad to want to sleep in tents anyway; we were, as we told each other, there for the riding not the camping and so we gave in. The rooms were simple but adequate; iron bedsteads, a concrete floor covered in dust and cigarette ends, bare walls, a naked light bulb hanging from the ceiling and a wooden table. In Europe they would pass for prison cells; here they represented luxury. A rusty wash bowl on a stand and a cracked mirror completed the amenities. We pulled the beds together and used our own bedding.

Mr Li said, 'This is a Chinese country hotel. Soon this area will be open to foreigners and they are getting ready.' 'We couldn't be more comfy,' said Louella bravely, but a quick look at the public latrines made us speculate how the first coachload of blue-rinsed ladies from Denver would react. There was a well in the yard from which we drew water for the horses and for ourselves. A mud brick outhouse was being built and we were told that the horses could spend the night there.

Mr He was allowed to cook in the corridor and as usual produced a masterpiece, this time almost entirely vegetarian. A friendly crowd came in to watch us eat and for good measure inspected our room and our possessions. Our crew, who were very security-conscious, kept shooing them out but we could see that they would never steal anything.

In the middle of the night we woke to the sound of pounding hooves and realized that the horses had escaped. Dragging on our trousers we ran to chase them. They were charging wildly around the courtyard, clearly enjoying themselves and in no mood to be caught. If they had got out of the yard we really might have had a problem, but fortunately the night watchman woke up in time to close the gates. Every time we came near them they charged straight at us, kicking up their heels and bucking. Only when they galloped into a side yard and stopped there to eat some of their hay, which I'd fetched, could we catch them, and then they were instantly as quiet as lambs. Normally they had nice natures and we were becoming fond of them. Tang would nicker at me in the morning when I gave him a lump of sugar. Ming did not like sugar, but he was gentle and willing when being ridden. Now we tied them to a clothes line, but soon afterwards Tang was seen undoing the knots with his teeth and we had to tie special ones to defeat him.

Ann Bridge's most famous book about China is *Peking Picnic*. Having read and enjoyed it, we had conceived the idea of having such a picnic ourselves for all our friends in Peking to celebrate the completion of the first stage of our ride which brought us back almost to the capital. We had even chosen the proposed site, a delightful cove on the Miyun Reservoir north of the city, and the long-suffering John Dennis had been given a list of people to invite once we knew when we would arrive there. It now looked as though we would make it by the following Sunday, barring accidents, and as this was of course the perfect day for people to come we were anxious to get word to John as soon as possible. There was a telephone in Banbishan, but getting through to Peking took several hours and when finally the Embassy was on the line, they could not hear us at all. Shouting myself hoarse I yelled, 'Miyun Sunday,' again and again until I got what sounded like an acknowledgement and we were cut off.

Now we were free to enjoy the rest of our day off. Taking our books we headed north from the village on a track leading up a promising valley. After a couple of miles we came to an even better view than those of the previous day. We looked over a ridge on to Shangri La. Climbing up through pine woods, we found a shady place where we could sit in dappled sunlight and observe the wonderful valley below us. In a great bowl in the mountains lay a cultivated hill, which seemed surrounded like an island by a wide loop of river. On either side bridges led to small villages nestling in their trees and all over the hill the work plots and crops were like a patchwork on the fertile soil. With water – the lifeblood of China – everywhere it looked to be an idyllic place. All around were the Yan Shan mountains and stillness. We were at least 1,000 feet above the valley floor, but voices carried up to us and every now and then the frogs in the river would set up a chorus of croaking. A cuckoo, which the Chinese call buku, was calling from across the valley and yellow swallow-tailed butterflies drifted past. As we lay and read it was impossible to imagine anywhere we would rather be.

The valley seemed to represent China at its very best. Virtually self-sufficient, indeed prosperous by most Third World standards, it was as neatly and artistically laid out as a painting. Tempting rough

This cultivated valley in the Yan Shan mountains seemed to us to represent rural China at its very best.

tracks which someone else can explore one day led off into the wooded valleys. Originally the Wall ran along the northern boundary of civilization, which meant good land. Often, indeed, it was carefully built along the watershed to deprive the barbarians of access to the sources of southward flowing rivers. I had not realized that we would see such good land outside the Wall; there was a palpable air of contentment there. Even the large black ants which climbed all over us and investigated us thoroughly failed to bite.

After a couple of hours we climbed to the top of the nearest hill, where the sun beat down on baking rocks, and sunbathed for a while. When the heat became too great we climbed down by a steep path through some terraced fields where a friendly man with a large yellow dog was inspecting some recently planted fruit trees.

As we neared Banbishan we fell in with three charming schoolgirls walking home. They looked much younger, but told us in quite good English that they were sixteen. We invited them to come and call on us later and they left us giggling uncontrollably. Back in the yard we washed in buckets of cold water from the well and felt a lot better for it. Afterwards we went for an evening stroll through the village. Perhaps because we had been there for a whole day and by then everyone knew who we were and what we were doing, we felt that we were stared at less and instead people smiled at us and even greeted us with an occasional 'Ni hao'. There was a nice relaxed atmosphere and we began to tell ourselves that it might be possible for foreigners to be invisible in China. But the moment we went into the village shop we realized how wrong we were. It was quite a large store and completely empty when we entered. By the time we had walked the length of the long counter and looked at a few items we did not need, the shop was full and we had to fight our way out through an eager crowd. We hoped for the shopkeeper's sake that perhaps they bought something.

During supper, for which Mr He had obtained some small river fish which he cooked whole – heads, tails, insides and all – our three schoolgirls arrived with eight friends. They watched us eat for a while which they found interesting and then we showed them pictures of our baby, which reduced them to a state of total collapse. Eventually Madam Hao lost patience with them and sent them home. We gave the horses some exercise, as they had been standing about all day. We walked and trotted them around the compound and were relieved to see that Tang was no longer lame.

The hotel 'proprietor' was a charming old boy with whom we had a long session settling up our minuscule bill. His unredeeming feature was that he was a master spitter. Suddenly, in the middle of an amiable conversation, he would clear his throat ominously, roll the resulting phlegm around his mouth for a bit and then carefully drop it on the floor next to his chair. Later, when we were sitting with our crew having a last mug of tea before turning in, I felt a sneeze coming on and pulled a big red-spotted handkerchief from my pocket. After sneezing I blew my nose loudly and as I did so I caught sight of kind, motherly Madam Hao's face. Reflected in her appalled expression I saw exactly the same disgust which had been on Louella's face when the old man spat. It was salutary to realize that my actions were just as offensive in Chinese eyes and there are no absolute or universal standards of behaviour.

6

PEKING PICNIC

very evening Madam Hao was there to greet us, clapping her hands, with a big smile on her plump face. As we eased ourselves out of the saddle she always said, with genuine concern in her voice, that we must be tired: 'Robin lei la, Louella lei la.' Then she would clasp Louella to her ample bosom for a comforting hug. Her equanimity was only shaken when her precious minibus was disturbed by dirt, damage or other vehicles. Dangerous drivers were threatened with a shake of her massive fist, and our sacks of horse feed were not popular as they tended to leak onto the floor. I feared for her suspension and peace of mind because the road west from Banbishan was terrible. Often it consisted of nothing more than piles of unbroken boulders and the only other traffic we saw was an occasional heavy lorry carrying stones.

We climbed steadily up into the mountains beside a rocky river, now low but clearly at times a mighty torrent. Ducks dabbled in the shallows and the sun shone from a clear blue sky. The scenery became wilder as we gained altitude. From a distance the mountains could have been anywhere, but once we were in among them there was a peculiar cragginess, with wild mad pinnacles of rock and eccentric beautiful pines leaning into space from unlikely crevices, which stamped them as unmistakably Chinese. Without having ever visited a Chinese mountain before, I felt I would have known that this was China if I had been transported there blindfold.

The rocks of the cliff faces were very strange. Riddled with horizontal and vertical cracks of a reddish brown, they looked like slabs of dried cork. A lot of quarrying was going on, as it seems to all over China, the stone being used for the road, for terracing and to build groins in the river bed. A couple of times dynamite exploded without warning quite close to us. The horses were good and calm; perhaps as military horses they had heard loud bangs before. Apart from these disturbances we saw few people during the day. For once there were no donkey carts and often we were alone for long periods without even a bicyclist.

High up, where the river bed was dry and such water as there was flowed underground most of the time, Louella spotted a perfect place for our midday rest. In a patch of vivid green marsh a cool fresh spring welled up and flowed for a yard or two before vanishing again below the rounded boulders of the river. We and the horses drank from this and then, because they were so clearly enthusiastic about grazing the lush grass, we let them loose, hoping they would not try to escape. For once we had no visitors and could sleep peacefully in the sun.

At the top of the pass the road went through a tunnel and I wondered how the horses would react. But they were quite unafraid of the dark and even when, inevitably, one of the rare lorries came through just as we were in the middle, they paid no attention and kept to the side. Outside in the sunshine again we began a steep and zigzag descent towards Xinglong. This was the one place specifically mentioned in our military permit that we must ride around and not through. Of course we wondered what we were not supposed to see and looked around all the more keenly. As we approached the town we saw some very strange buildings high on a hill to the north and surrounded by a high wall. There were two gleaming observatories, their domes shining in the sun, and next to them a tall tower. Perhaps that was it.

In the next village we paused to watch two young women having a noisy and quite violent fight surrounded by an interested crowd. One was screaming abuse at the other at the top of her voice while trying to grab her hair or punch her. But the moment we were noticed everything stopped and all attention, including that of the two combatants, was directed at us. At that moment a small motorized tricycle with a cab pulled up and two important-looking military men got out of the back. The senior one was very severe. Sternly he held up his hand to stop us and indicated that we should dismount. This we chose not to understand. Then he waved his blue identity card at us and signalled that he wanted to see ours. Although we did not have our passports on us we did fortunately have the Aliens' Travel Permit which named all the places on our route. He scrutinized this carefully, found Xinglong on it, to his evident surprise, and returned it to us. When we showed him one of our handouts he became positively friendly, saluted and waved us on. This was the only time on the whole ride that we were stopped and asked for our papers.

The road went past Xinglong and so it was not necessary to enter the forbidden centre. As we rode along we could see a large, grim camp with wooden towers at the corners, barbed wire and rows of long huts. A labour camp or top security prison, perhaps, we thought. But when we asked Mr Li what there was in Xinglong that was so secret, he said that the only reason we had been told to avoid the centre of town was because it was being rebuilt and so was in a dreadful mess.

We camped a short way beyond the town and that night Mr He demonstrated his Kung Fu skills to us. He had extraordinary control over his body as he performed the balletic ritual associated with this martial art. He was able to fall to the floor like a log and he could lie rigid between two chairs, supported only by his neck and ankles, for an indefinite time.

Mr Li was forty and therefore still a student when the Cultural Revolution broke out in 1966. He had been a Red Guard and forbidden to study for nine years. Instead he had rampaged around the country with a group who harangued the people with extracts from Mao's *Little Red Book*. 'We were gripped by a kind of madness,' he said. As he had an extraordinarily loud voice, especially when nervous, he must have been good at it. But nonetheless he had studied English secretly, rightly thinking that it might come in useful one day. Most of the rest of his generation are totally uneducated. The skilled and those in authority today are nearly all much older or younger.

We asked Madam Hao how she had fared at that time and she replied that as her husband was in the army they had not done too badly. The military stood apart during the Cultural Revolution and they were virtually the only section of the community safe from the attentions of the Red Guards. Now everyone seemed to talk quite openly about those dreadful days, comparing notes on their sufferings, vying with each other over stories of being sent to live in caves or being separated from husband or wife for the decade. Many are still separated.

We slept in a village called Huangjiaguan, which means the place of yellow wine. Before Liberation this was a prime fruit growing area, but because there were no roads then the crop used to be allowed to rot on the ground and the smell was like fermenting wine, so they told us. We had a room with a hard straw mattress on which we slept fitfully, disturbed by the horses stamping restlessly all night outside. A very long and tiring day lay ahead of us.

During the morning Tang began to go lame again and both horses needed constant urging to prevent them walking slower and slower. After a time the road was metal and there were fewer stretches where we could canter along the verge. Our bones ached and we devised ways of distracting ourselves from painful reality. One was to test each other on Chinese verbs and phrases, another to tell long stories of books or films only one of us had read or seen. Fortunately we both talk a lot and are never bored in each other's company. We also tried hard to observe and identify the birds, trees and flowers we saw along the way. Here larks were nearly always present, singing their way up into the clear blue sky or feeding on the ground beside us. They were bigger than the ones at home and had pronounced crests. Sometimes, as we approached a village, one of the less attractive features of modern China would suddenly compete with their song. Even in the remotest villages we saw loudspeakers mounted on a water tower or other high point, and when music or exhortations to work harder and love China were broadcast through them the din could be heard for miles. Often the distortion was so great that it was hard to tell if the music was Chinese or western. Fortunately most were not in use and we had the feeling that the people were beginning to tire of the constant deluge of propaganda to which they had been subjected for so long. However, even if this is so, the political slogans and hearty martial music will probably only be replaced by local pop music played just as loud, as already happens in so much of the Third World. Most villages had some electricity, usually just a handful of 40-watt bulbs, but few had more than a single tap to supply water and mostly this was fetched from the river or a well, in buckets suspended across the shoulders. The communal latrines were always dry and with a pigsty alongside. Inside the houses had floors of beaten earth or sometimes concrete and the family usually slept on brick platforms with a stove called a kang underneath which could, in the depths of winter, be fired with twigs, straw or animal dung. Sometimes a heating flue led inside the house from a cooking stove outside.

Some of the time we walked to spare the horses as the road climbed and dropped through a series of ridges. Once again the most memorable moment of the day was our midday rest. It seemed impossible that we would be able to improve on the ideal picnic sites we had already stumbled on, but this time we were simply dazzled by a brilliant little meadow of splendid buttercups in a grove of poplars. The horses were too exhausted by the heat and the steepness of the ascent to do more than roll and then stay lying down, barely bothering to graze. We lay and munched on biscuits and dried prunes while bright red ladybirds with no spots landed all over us. Thinking that the colours were almost too good to be true we looked up into the shimmering green and silver of the poplars and saw two lovely golden orioles mobbing a magpie which had dared come too close to their nest. As they swooped past the buttercups they became invisible against them. A tiny grey and black striped squirrel, no more than six inches long, flicked its tail over its back and sat up to eat a nut held in its front paws; grey wagtails bobbed and dipped on the rocks and a cuckoo called persistently from the hills. It must be said that most of the time the landscape was dry and brown, which only made these rare lush midday moments all the more memorable. Also spring is, I suspect, the only time of year when there is much colour to be seen in these hills.

We thought the afternoon would never end as we dragged ourselves and our tired animals towards Miyun. By the time we arrived, met up with our crew and then managed to get lost and wasted a couple of hours going in the wrong direction, we had covered 47 miles (75 kilometres) and we had been on the road for over 13 hours. We spent the night in a billet owned by the local work brigade, where they provided accommodation for farmers and drovers coming into town with their produce. It was more like a Middle-Eastern caravanserai; a spacious yard where a great many mules and donkeys were being fed and watered while their masters lounged about smoking or cooked in their cell-like quarters around the sides. There were good mangers and sturdy hitching posts and it was a relief to be staying somewhere where our mode of transport at least was not considered extraordinary. In the morning we were woken by a cock crowing. There was a great bustle as teams were harnessed to their carts and departed to loud cracks of whips and cries of 'huh', which with only the slightest tonal variation meant either right or left.

It took us less than three hours to ride by the side of a busy highway from Miyun to the reservoir on the fringes of the city. On the way we passed an amusement park, which had just been completed, for the entertainment of the people of Peking. In it was a huge roller coaster with its first screaming passengers of the day being terrified right next to the road. Nothing could have been more incongruous after the wild landscape we had been riding through. There was even a papier maché Great Wall around the entrance with the real thing only a couple of miles away.

At the reservoir, a vast and beautiful lake with islands and a backcloth of mountains, where the Great Wall is silhouetted along the horizon, we found our secluded cove and set about cleaning up our picnic site. There was a rusty old iron boat to which we tied the horses and an amazing amount of litter as well as broken bottles, but we soon had it looking pristine and we were undisturbed except for a couple of fishermen on the headland. We made the crew, who clearly had no faith in the whole crazy affair, put up the tent and start cooking delicious titbits for our guests. We groomed the horses, cleaned our tack and our boots, and wrote a sign saying Peking Picnic. This we nailed to the tree where the track to our beach led off the road.

By midday we were convinced that our message had not been understood and that no one would come even if it had been. We sat in our chairs feeling ridiculous while Mr He piled more and more food up in front of us. Then Mickey Grant walked round the corner and said, 'Hi, welcome back!' He told us Robbie had hired a Cadillac and was on his way down. A huge black limousine with a futuristic television aerial on the back inched itself on to the beach and out poured about ten people carrying bottles of champagne, beer, white wine, and maotai – the Chinese spirit in which toasts are given. Soon afterwards Richard and Grania Evans, their children and Grania's parents, who were of an age to have been at the original picnic in the 1920s, arrived in the Embassy Daimler flying the Union flag, followed by several

Our modern Peking picnic on the shore of the Miyun Reservoir. We had now completed the first stage of our ride, having ridden back to near Peking from the coast.

more cars, until a very noisy party was under way. With the relief of having arrived and our first alcoholic drink for some time we were soon both pretty merry, but we energetically tacked up the horses so that everyone could get pictures of us riding them. Then we gave virtually everyone present a go. This included many of the Chinese officials who had helped us get permission for the ride. Tang and Ming behaved themselves immaculately, plodding up and down the hill beneath riders of all shapes and sizes. I gave a rather incoherent interview to Mark Brayne, the BBC man in Peking, whose whole delightful family had come with him, and then I sold Tang. This was the end of the first stage of our journey and we would need to buy new horses at a point where we were to be allowed to start again. A good friend called Peter Batey, after four years as Edward Heath's secretary, had just come to Peking as the accountants Arthur Anderson's representative. He was living in the Great Wall Hotel and I convinced him that he would go mad in that unreal atmosphere unless he had an activity which took him out of town regularly. What better than a horse? We gave Ming to Robbie in gratitude for all he had done. He said he would keep both horses on a farm just outside the city where all were welcome to come and ride them. It was a very good party and the afternoon slipped by as the drink which everyone had brought was consumed and Mr He's food was appreciated. 'With a cook like this you must have had an easy time,' everyone said, and we agreed that it had all been glorious so far.

John Dennis had even arranged a truck to take the horses into Peking. This was just a small open lorry with a couple of bits of scaffolding tied along the sides. When it backed into a bank and we led the horses round, they just walked straight on without protest. During the fast drive along the motorway into town we followed behind, astonished at how calm they were under circumstances it seemed unlikely they had had to face before. Side by side in the open air they ignored the traffic hurtling past and only revealed their nervousness in the way they leant into each other for security and companionship. On arrival at the stable where they were to spend a couple of nights they had to jump straight down off the back, which they did without a murmur.

Our triumphal return to the Jianguo Hotel, where we had spent so much time worrying if we would ever leave, was great fun. The staff were not used to guests arriving in their elegant lobby extremely travel-stained, wearing riding boots and carrying large saddles. Our camping gear and cooking equipment contrasted oddly with the immaculate bags of the pretty Lufthansa stewardesses checking in beside us. The senior staff took it all in their well-trained stride and welcomed us back, but the porters, who were not used to handling sacks and saddles, were supercilious and allowed us to manhandle the trolley ourselves along to the storeroom.

We were in far too good a mood to allow anything to deflate us and the party continued as different friends came and went. Robbie had arrived, of course, and was entertaining Alan and Eileen Bond, who had just flown in from Australia with their Prime Minister on an official visit.

With them were David Davies, the handsome head of Hong Kong Land, and so ultimately responsible for our food from Dairy Farm, with his glamorous wife Linda. Later we all dined together and celebrated until the small hours in Charlie's Bar. Although our purpose in being there was to experience rural China it was good for Louella's morale to be feeling clean and pretty again.

Much the hardest part of our journey lay ahead; but we had proved it was possible to ride in China and we now felt confident that we would reach the end of the Wall.

7

DETOUR IN XIAN

*B*ursting with energy to sort everything out and be on our way again, I jogged with Robbie before breakfast and swam ten lengths of the hotel pool. There was a lot to do and every reason to delay for further protracted negotiations, but I was determined that we must keep moving. Our various host organizations begged us to spend some time getting more permissions, but I insisted that we would catch the train to our next starting point in three days. My most fervently observed rule of travel is that the longer a traveller stays in a city the more things will turn up which he will have to sort out before he can leave.

We talked to the press and bought our train tickets. We had our second Japanese encephalitis injections at the Embassy, collected a pile of letters and wrote replies. We had my camera repaired and decided to buy a spare for Louella to use as her own. From then on she took the black and white while I took the colour photographs. We whizzed around the town on bicycles, shopping and seeing people. I had lost a filling and was given the name of a lady professor at the dental hospital who was highly recommended by the Embassy. It was a huge place where no one spoke English and explaining one's needs by sign language was alarming. Through countless doors off endless corridors were rows and rows of dentists' chairs where men and women in white coats and masks were hard at work on open mouths. It was like being in a hall of mirrors. A kind nurse took me under her wing, filled out the necessary forms from guesswork and delivered me to the professor, who drilled and filled expertly.

Back at the hotel we met Mickey, who was deeply depressed at receiving in writing a definite refusal of permission to film our ride. We showed it to Robbie, who said, 'That's excellent. Now we know they are about to give in!' He also told us that an item about our ride had appeared in *Reference News* and this should help us greatly. *Reference News* is a tabloid containing selected items of news about international and Chinese events filched from the foreign press. Foreigners are not allowed to see it, probably because it might give them an insight into

Chinese preoccupations, but it is claimed to be the most widely read paper in the world with ten million copies printed daily, each copy seen by perhaps fifteen people. Now we learned that it had picked up the Reuters' report of our departure from Shanhaiguan.

Our last evening in Peking provided the ultimate in Chinese contrasts. We dined on the terrace of the Embassy Residence by candlelight. Above us glowed red lanterns and a moon; we were served exquisite food by silent and efficient Chinese staff. The guests were cultivated and cosmopolitan. They toasted Grania's birthday and made witty speeches. But we had to leave before the end to deal with our baggage, which had to be sent by goods train to Xian. There were twenty-three pieces, all our supplies and equipment for the rest of our time in China; far too much to go in the compartment with us. We had been told that the quietest time for checking it in at the station would be 11 p.m. and that was when we arrived.

There were slightly fewer people than when we had bought our tickets earlier, but the scene which greeted us still resembled the aftermath of a nuclear holocaust. Bodies lay everywhere, singly and in heaps. One group of ten lay like the spokes of a wheel, their heads resting on their baggage piled in the centre. We had to park a long way from the freight hall and pick our route through. Then our troubles began. There were no porters or trolleys and the official in charge was extremely unfriendly. Each item had to be carried by hand between us over the sleeping crowds. When we finally had everything stacked up in the hall, he said it was improperly packaged. The trunks must have padlocks, the sacks must be stitched and the boxes tied with stronger cord. The people who could be paid to see to the packaging had gone home. It was now 11.15 p.m., the office closed at 11.30 p.m. and quite clearly we were in an impossible predicament where disaster loomed. These situations occur all too often in China; in fact travel seems to revolve round them. The traveller, and to be fair it seems to make no difference if you are Chinese or foreign, is driven to despair by insuperable problems and it is tempting to rant and rave. But it is essential to stay calm and polite, outwardly determined against all odds to succeed somehow. Suddenly what we came to call the First Night Syndrome would come into effect. In a flash everything changes and a glimmer of light appears at the end of the tunnel. From being surly and unhelpful, those around are transformed into the most friendly, inventive and helpful people on earth.

A girl in blue uniform produced a needle and began speedily stitching up our sacks. Three new padlocks appeared and were paid for by me without a murmur. Sixty-nine labels (three for each item) were written out and stamped at the speed of light. A couple of items we had been told at first were quite unacceptable – a bundle of chairs for example – suddenly became invisible and were passed through.

The office did not close and by midnight all was finished. As we shook hands all round and thanked everyone for their kindness, the formerly surly boss said with a broad grin that he had read all about us in *Reference News* and hoped we would have a good ride.

For the 24-hour journey to Xian we shared our soft sleeper compartment with a serene old general of temperate habits, who neither smoked nor spat. Messrs Li and He, who were to stay with us the whole way, were in the next compartment and so we only saw them for meals. Madam Hao had driven us to the station for our morning departure and promised to collect us again wherever we arrived back. We hoped to arrange fresh transport and a new driver in Xian.

The weather was now very hot both day and night, and we had sweated copiously loading our baggage the night before and again fighting our way on to the train. Now we sweltered as it made its way across the plains of Hebei. It was a chance to read, write and sleep. Once we started to climb up into the mountains of Shanxi, the scenery became much more interesting and the train wound along the edge of deep valleys and passed through numerous tunnels. They were rugged, dry mountains, but with lots of terraces irrigated from clear rivers, groves of poplars and dirt roads. Excellent riding country, we thought. The character of the houses and villages had changed completely. No more the uniform 'railway carriage' design, they now reminded me more of Arab hill towns, the houses being made of mud and stone, clustered together one above the other. But the arches of the doors and windows were Norman rather than Byzantine, rounded rather than pointed.

We awoke in Shaanxi province to completely different countryside: lush, undulating hills and river plains where rich market gardening was being carried out on the farmland. The fertile Wei River valley, through which we approached Xian, was the cradle of Chinese civilization. Populated as early as 6000 BC, in Neolithic times, some of the first agriculture in the world was practised here.

We were met at the station by contacts arranged through CITIC and an official of the railway who guided us across the tracks, between four big steam engines puffing away, to a special exit. This was, he said, 'to avoid the crowds and some reporters'. It was a welcome change not to be pushing and fighting our way through the throng and we followed them docilely. They had put us in the Bell Tower Hotel, which is right in the centre of town, overlooking the Bell Tower which is the symbol of the city. The view from the window was the hotel's only redeeming feature. Described in one of our guide books as resembling a compartmentalized aircraft hangar and in the other as new but deteriorating, it was perfectly adequate, but nothing worked, everything was very dirty and the staff seemed to have been specially trained in the art of unhelpfulness.

Here we had planned to spend two nights but, due to further delays over permits and a resolute refusal all round to let us move until they came through, we were doomed to be stuck for eight. There are many worse places to be stuck than Xian, as there is a great deal to see, including some of the great wonders of the world, but we fretted because our time in China was running out and we still had a very long way to go. Meanwhile, we became very privileged sightseers as our transport was produced and a reasonable price agreed for it on the first day. It was a 20-seater bus, which comfortably took all our baggage. In it we could visit the sights at our leisure and in our own time, thus avoiding the coachloads of foreign and Chinese tourists.

Most important for us were the tomb of the Emperor Qin and the terracotta figures guarding it. Everyone now knows the story of how in 1974 peasants digging a well uncovered what is now recognized as one of the greatest archaeological finds ever made. Thousands of life-sized figures of warriors and their horses drawn up in battle formation were buried a mile or so from the tomb, a whole army ready to protect their Emperor, and these are gradually being excavated. Over the main site a vast roof has been built to protect it from the elements. At other sites, more figures, including horses and chariots, were found. These have been filled in again with soil to protect them for future excavations.

Under the roof six thousand life-size figures stand or kneel in serried ranks. Each has different features and clothing. Moustaches and hairstyles can only have been modelled from life. Some smile, some scowl; some have loose scarves around their necks, others what look like cravats. They wear loose-fitting robes or, in the case of horsemen, short coats of chain mail and wind-proof caps. Many hold real weapons, which have been removed from the thousand or so already excavated. The rest lie buried under the yellow earth. Heads and torsos emerge from test holes which reveal the size of the site. The first thing which struck me about them was how nice and amiable they all looked; good companions and loyal friends, gentlemen who enjoyed life rather than representatives of one of the most powerful and irresistible armies ever. They were never intended to be seen as they are now exposed. They were there, beautifully painted in colours which are now fading, standing in their rows in dark passages under low roofs, an incredible invisible presence below the ground, unknown for century after century. We gazed and wondered, unmindful of the other tourists who arrived, the garish notices, the prohibitions in English against taking photographs, the noise of engines and voices. A scene too grandiose for the mind to grasp is being revealed.

Some workers, mostly women in padded overalls, were hacking away at the central terraces and loading soil into a dumper truck. As it chugged off up a ramp we could feel the vibration it caused under our feet and clods of earth fell down into the pit where the immaculate soldiers stood. The women smoked and rested on their shovels, chattering and flicking their stubs away. It all seemed so casual. The figures which had been exposed looked clean and well preserved, but many had broken arms or heads and we wondered if this damage had ever been caused by a carelessly swung pickaxe rather than time. We felt that there must be more sophisticated techniques now for sucking dust and dirt away gently rather than the crude methods being used. We were both delighted and appalled by what we saw that day. In a way our feelings at that most celebrated of Chinese exhibits were similar to those we came to feel about China in general.

The figures are wonderful, but they are, however, only an appendage of the real treasure house. It is the promise of what is yet to come which is most exciting about the place. The Emperor Qin, which is pronounced Chin, gave his name to China. When he was crowned King of Qin in 247 BC at the age of thirteen work began on his mausoleum, 700,000 castrated men labouring on a construction 4 miles (6 kilometres) in girth. This continued for the next thirty-six years of his reign, during which he conquered and unified China to become its first emperor. His tomb lies beneath a man-made hill a mile from the site of the terracotta army. It has not yet been excavated and may never have been looted. If so, unimaginable treasures await archaeologists underneath the 150 foot (46 metre) high mound which covers the tomb. Historical records exist which describe an amazing subterranean palace, a microcosm of the world, and recent measurements indicate that they may be no exaggeration.

The walls of the tomb itself are said to be lined with bronze plates to keep the water out. Liquid mercury was pumped in to create underground rivers and oceans, which could be made to flow and surge. Pearls and jewels studded the ceiling to make galaxies of stars while gold and silver ducks and wild geese were placed on the floor among jade pine trees. An entire imperial court with palaces and pavilions filled with treasures and utensils for the afterworld was reproduced to accompany the Emperor for eternity. And at the end all those who had worked to build it and all the palace maids were buried alive with him, so that none could reveal its secrets. It is also said to be guarded by crossbows set to impale intruders automatically. Since the bronze weapons held by the terracotta figures were found to have been treated with special rust-resistant material so that after more than 2,000 years they were still sharp, the first archaeologists to penetrate the site should be wary. And this is what worries me about the whole future of the site. The Chinese, the heirs to those who created all the treasures, find it hard to accept that any modern barbarian could have anything to contribute to their excavation. We were told that no foreign scientists have been allowed to take part in the work, in spite of offers from universities around the world who would be happy to contribute money, personnel and expertise in return simply for the interest of being there. Doubtless the Chinese do have good archaeologists, though their numbers must have been depleted during the Cultural Revolution when such occupations were considered bourgeois and revisionist. They say they will excavate slowly and it may be decades before the whole complex and the tomb itself is uncovered, and this sounds sensible, except for the nagging suspicion that they may be doing it wrong. It is such a unique world treasure that the very best world experts should surely be allowed to help. The memory of that dumper truck impacting the soil, and the labourers hacking away with pickaxes inches from the terracotta figures while stubbing their cigarettes out on them haunts me. Besides, if they take that long I may not still be around to see what is in the tomb when it is finally opened.

The museums around the site were quite well done with clear signs and a lot of interesting information. The models of horses which had been restored were also excellent. At first they looked stylized but on closer inspection we could see that each was different and had its own character. They were not shod, all seemed to be geldings and they stood nearly 15 hands, as tall as any horses we had seen in modern China. A beautiful bronze chariot with four horses and a kneeling coachman, perhaps charged with carrying the Emperor on his long journey through the heavens, had recently been unearthed. Everything was in astonishing condition, the trappings, reins and decorations gleaming brightly. They reminded me of the four bronze chargers above the central portal of St Mark's Basilica in Venice. Those were cast during Nero's reign in Rome three hundred years later and are rather more lively and naturalistic. It does seem extraordinary that two of the most beautiful quartets of bronze horses known throughout history should have been made so relatively close together in time and so very far apart in distance.

We climbed through pomegranate bushes, their flowers a gaudy red and orange, to the top of the hill above the Emperor's tomb. Behind, the mountains towered up with dramatic terracing and high alpine meadows visible. Below, the lush countryside with fields of green wheat, some just beginning to turn yellow, was broken by copses and gave a surprising feel of Wiltshire in the summer.

At the foot of the hill was a double row of stalls run by delightfully aggressive ladies. They looked and behaved like gypsies, thrusting their wares under our noses, shrieking with laughter at our bargaining, a marvellous contrast to the usual dour state stores. The goods on offer were also astonishingly varied and colourful. Since we were the centre of so much attention, there being no other tourists around, and therefore in a strong position to haggle, we decided it was as good an opportunity as any to buy some presents for our family. There were lots of dazzlingly embroidered children's clothes as well as old silk garments in need of some repair but of excellent quality. We bought our baby son a padded scarlet suit covered in dragons for the equivalent of a couple of pounds sterling and a beautiful antique waistcoat. Everything was ridiculously cheap. The accurate scale models of the terracotta soldiers had been for sale in the museum at £7–£20. Here they were 50p or so and just as well made. It was good to see how the little bit of free enterprise allowed there to satisfy the tourist trade had sparked off a boom in the local economy. These people were responding accurately to what the foreigners who came from all over the world to see the excavations wanted to buy and they were manufacturing it, doubtless including the antiques, at prices which were irresistible.

We later discussed this phenomenon with our crew, who had at the time seemed rather shocked by the aggressive commercialism displayed by these traders. I tried to explain how refreshing I found their cheerfulness and enthusiasm after the surly salesmanship in state shops. To our surprise they agreed, saying, 'No competition, no progress.'

The sights of Xian kept us occupied for the next week as we tried not to let the delays exasperate us. It is a city with a cheerful relaxed atmosphere where one can stroll among the street vendors. Food, ice cream and trinkets of all sorts are sold from handcarts by peddlers. One man had a large set of scales, such as are seen sometimes in chemists, on which one could be weighed for a small sum. Another had his bicycle almost concealed under cages of budgerigars. In the Moslem quarter of Xian around the Great Mosque narrow streets run between old houses. Enterprising shopkeepers had their colourful wares outside for visiting Chinese and the occasional foreign tourist. The mosque itself, one of the largest in China, was a haven of peace in the bustling city. The gardens and buildings are Chinese in style but there was a deep sense of reverence there, untarnished for once by any young sneering Party members. Instead sedate gentlemen in turbans strolled among the roses and the birdsong looking pensive and for the first time in China we felt that here were people who were not afraid of being devout. The services were well attended by up to 2,000 of the 30,000 Moslems in Xian and a major rebuilding programme was under way, financed, we were told, by the Aga Khan. Before the Cultural Revolution there were fourteen mosques in Xian; now there are three or four, but Islam is regaining the ground lost then, when all Moslem privileges were removed for a time. The mosque was founded in AD 742, when Arab traders reached Xian. Later it was to become the dominant faith in much of northern China and was adopted by many of the ethnic minorities. As a result Moslems have suffered less from repression than Christians since the revolution, because there has always been a danger of their violent resistance.

Our visit to the zoo was a far less agreeable experience. Fortunately we went alone, as our disgust was such that we would not have been able to restrain ourselves from being uncivil to our hosts and crew about the conditions in which the animals were kept. The site was attractive enough, with water, willows and low hills, but almost all the enclosures were mean and bare, the animals miserable. Mangy wolves and foxes, their ribs showing and with sores on their legs, paced around slatted cages, their feet slipping between the bars. They stank and looked wretched, while the shouting Chinese visitors threw stones at them and flapped their arms for a reaction. It would have done no good to intervene. Everywhere we looked there were injured animals and birds. The camel house was a bedlam of hysterical filthy beasts, moulting great mats of hair and galumphing insanely about. The deer stared into space, emaciated and sick, scouring, dying. Between the animals were noisy circus and funfair exhibits, a roundabout with blaring music and a wall of death where motorcycles roared about.

A large notice proclaimed 'a super animal star, a living fossil'. For an extra 3 yuan we could see Dan Dan, the brown and white panda caught the year before in Shaanxi province. Poor Dan Dan. She lay in a tiny cage on bare concrete, alone and bored with nothing to do but hang her paws through the bars and try to get comfortable. A giggling crowd, which she ignored, tossed coins and cigarette packets at her. Her septum had been ripped through and stuck out pinkly from the middle of her nose, giving her an air of infinite tragedy. There was nothing we could do.

Avenues or 'spirit ways' of giant stone animals and human figures leading to tombs, some with accompanying museums, abound within driving distance of Xian. With our own transport we were able to visit several and to see a lot of the countryside at the same time. Of them all our favourites were two tombs near the burial place of the third Tang Emperor Gaozang, known as the Qian tomb. One was the tomb of Princess Yongtai, where deep underground in a cool, dank tunnel were wonderfully vivid paintings of life at the Tang court. Comely ladies in stylish gowns, whose pure colours were still bright after 1,200 years, moved gracefully about, smiling. They were carrying offerings of fruit and food in bowls and cloths, and they were impeccably coiffed. Life at the Tang court must have been very civilized but also very danger- ous. Princess Yongtai had been executed by her grandmother the Empress Wu on suspicion of having criticized one of her cronies. During the seventh century China was ruled, as happened quite often, by a powerful, scheming woman. Wu Zetian had been a concubine of Taizong, the second Tang Emperor, who had died in AD 649 when she was only twenty-five years old. For a time she had become a Buddhist nun until recalled by Gaozong, the old Emperor's ninth son, to be first his concubine too and then in 655 (at thirty-one) his Empress. When he died she managed, through palace intrigue and murder, to dispose

A large saddled horse on a spirit way near Xian. Originally a stone groom would have stood beside it.

of two of her own sons and in 690 (aged sixty-six) to rule as the Empress Wu until she was over eighty, when she was finally deposed.

One of her sons was the heir apparent, Prince Zhanghuai, whom she forced to commit suicide in disgrace. His tomb, the second of our favourites, also contained beautiful murals along the walls of the subterranean passage leading down to the sarcophagus. These were of horsemen playing polo and hunting, a marvellous assortment of animals riding with them. Perched behind them or clasped in their arms were hawks, owls, dogs and even a leopard as they careered through the trees having a tremendous time.

In Teresa Waugh's translation of *The Travels of Marco Polo* there is a description which mirrors this scene uncannily. It also echoes Coleridge's poem and I wonder if he had read a version of it and whether it surfaced in his subconscious when he dreamt 'Kubla Khan'. Had he not been interrupted by 'a person on business from Porlock' we might have had a hunting scene in the poem.

LXXXV: THE CITY OF XANADU AND THE GREAT KHAN'S FABU-LOUS PALACE A further three days' ride takes the traveller to a city named Xanadu built for the present Great Khan, Kublai Khan. Here there is a stone and marble palace with gilded rooms wonderfully decorated with magnificent and delicate paintings of birds, trees and flowers of every kind. Leading away from the palace is a wall which encloses sixteen miles of fertile ground with rivers and streams running through it. Here the Great Khan rears every sort of animal, including fallow deer and roebuck which are fed to the many gerfalcons and falcons, and at least once a week he goes to look at them. He often rides through these gardens with a leopard squatting on his horse's hindquarters. Sometimes he unleashes the leopard and sends it to catch a deer or a roebuck for his falcons. This is a pastime much enjoyed by the Great Khan.

Although Marco Polo visited China six hundred years after these tombs were built, life at court does not seem to have changed very much. Certainly it was never more cosmopolitan than during the Tang dynasty, when China experienced the greatest flowering of its arts. Chinese domination reached as far as Turkestan along the Silk Road. Painting, sculpture and poetry flourished as never before or since and, because of the cavalry upon which the security of the nation depended, the horse was portrayed everywhere as the king of the animals.

It was a golden age. Changan, the old capital close to modern Xian, was the most enlightened city in the world, only rivalled by the Baghdad of Harun al Rashid. China already had a population of about 53 million of whom 2 million lived in the capital, where the streets teemed with travellers. This was the time when Chinese influence on Japan was strongest and the cities of Nara and Kyoto were modelled on Changan. The best examples of Tang wooden architecture survive there today. Persian influence was strong and religious freedom was allowed, with Nestorian Christians vying for congregations with Manichaeans and Zoroastrians. Buddhism was, of course, dominant with dozens of great monasteries, and Islam was just arriving.

None of the paintings we saw in the tombs were in very good condition and we were worried by the condensation on the walls caused by the visitors and the way people were able to lean across the barrier and touch the paint. Irrationally photography was strictly forbidden in the museum, where artefacts in glass cases were unlikely to be damaged by flash, but here it was unrestricted.

Although it was still May, the harvest was well under way and the roads were being used for threshing. Everywhere we drove grain had been spread out so that the passing traffic would do what otherwise had to be done laboriously by hand. It amazed me that all the vehicles did not have straw wound around their axles and drive shafts as they ploughed through a continuous sea of grain, but no one seemed to mind. They still all drove flat out and the peasants winnowing with pitchforks between them had to leap clear. Beside the roads bullocks were pulling large carved stone rollers round and round threshing more grain, while the ears of barley or millet were crushed by heavy hand-operated millstones. We saw rape seed being milled also, and rice grew in paddy fields close to the rivers.

A bullock pulling a large stone roller to thresh out the grain. Often crops were also spread on the roads for passing lorries to drive over.

Back in Xian we climbed the two astonishing pagodas which still tower over the ancient walls and modern buildings of the city. They are in such good condition that it is hard to believe they were built in the seventh century, but the views from the top over the smog-ridden industrial sprawl is depressing. Billed as China's most famous pagodas, there are various legends to explain how they acquired their names; the Big Goose and the Little Goose. I like best the story of a group of pious vegetarian Buddhist monks who, although they were starving, refused to kill and eat a wild goose which miraculously dropped out of the sky beside them. The Big Goose is the largest, at 210 feet (64 metres), and the oldest, having been built in AD 652. It seems that a monk who had returned from a great pilgrimage to India tried to persuade the emperor to build a large stone stupa like those he had seen on his travels. The brick structure creating the familiar many-storeyed pagoda shape was a compromise which became the established pattern.

We were taken to a silk factory, doubtless a showpiece, where rows of girls stitched busily away making embroidered kimonos, tablecloths and cushion covers. Louella, who is a talented patchwork quilt-maker, was impressed by their skill, especially the hand embroidery using silk thread. Small samples of this work, about six inches

The Little Goose pagoda in Xian, completed in AD 707. Originally it had fifteen storeys but in 1556 it lost the top two in an earthquake.

square, were for sale at a giveaway price of 2 yuan each. Louella decided that if we could collect enough of them in suitable matching colours they could be made up into a fantastic quilt when we got home. After some calculations on size and design she explained that we wanted thirty different designs of four different colours: gold, blue, green and red. Once we had passed the inevitable 'mei you' they began to enter into the spirit of the thing and we pulled out drawers, piling up and separating silk pictures of birds, flowers, butterflies and people.

They kept assuring us that that was all they had, and we kept finding more. At last we had the correct set of one hundred and twenty and it was time to discuss the price. As a matter of principle I explained that for such an exceptionally large order, which might be repeated, there must be a substantial discount. The unit price was 2 yuan and they suggested we might like to pay 230 yuan. I said we should have twenty per cent off which would make the price about 190 yuan. The manager was sent for. He seemed appalled both by the mess we had made of his factory and our presumption in trying to lower the fixed price so far; then he astonished us by saying we could have the lot for 150 yuan, far less than we were offering. This worked out at about 30p for each embroidery and so we paid up without demur.

As time dragged on and we were still not allowed to leave we decided we needed exercise to take our minds off it. We asked our nice new driver, Mr Bo, a sturdy reliable man, to drive us up into the mountains south of Xian so that we could go for a long walk. Embarrassed, he told us that only Xian itself and the tourist sites around were 'open' to foreigners. The rest of the country was closed. There was, however, one beauty spot we could visit and so we agreed to go there. It was a lake on Mount Cuibua, the foot of which was about an hour's drive south of Xian.

We left Mr Bo to go in search of some lunch while we climbed up a well-trod path alongside a clear tumbling river. There was birdsong and an increasingly magnificent view as we gained height. Trees shaded our trail and under them sat entrepreneurs selling home-made squash, ice creams and even hot meals of noodles and soup. The sun beat down and there were few other people except occasional parties of noisy schoolchildren. It was steep and it took us an hour to reach the top. There we found a Buddhist shrine and a pleasing hill village of old houses where, it seemed, modernity had not yet penetrated as there was no road. An old man sat in the sun puffing on his pipe, his two grandsons turning a millstone beside him, while chickens pecked at the fallen chaff. Beyond was the lake, where steep hillsides plunged straight down into deep water. Some rowing boats were moored there and it was peaceful, almost deserted, and silent until suddenly a truly dreadful noise rent the air. A long-worn-out needle on a scratched record was relayed through a distorted loudspeaker to produce nothing but noise. It was, after all, a beauty spot and someone was determined to prove it in the Chinese way. We had to walk for another hour along the shore until we were out of earshot. There we found a plashing stream, where we could bathe, scooping the cold water over ourselves, and a patch of sand where we could lie in the sun.

The Buddhist monastery at Xingjiao, which we visited on the way back to Xian, was the most active we had seen. The Abbott is a member of the Conference of Chinese Buddhists and the refectory,

'An old man sat in the sun puffing on his pipe.'

which was laid ready to accommodate more than a dozen monks, was decorated like a Rotary Club dining room with fraternal Buddhist flags from all over the world. Set on a hill among pines the seventh-century pagodas and twelfth-century pavilions faced back towards the mountains we had just left. Their summits looked like clouds above the hazy plain.

That evening we received a faint call from Peking telling us we could leave Xian and return to the Wall. To celebrate our departure we went out to dinner at the luxury hotel which caters to the uppermost market of 'terracotta tourists'. Chinese food is wonderful, but it always comes all at once and has to be eaten as messily as possible, gristle and bones scattered all over the plastic table top. At best warm beer or sickly sweet squash accompanies the meal and there is no temptation to linger. The Golden Flower is Swedish-owned and superbly run by the Norwegian manager and his Swiss wife. We dined with them on outstanding French cooking, the last non-Chinese meal we would enjoy until our journey was over. Their Austrian chef had discovered quantities of *ecrevisses*, fresh water crayfish, in the market; crystal finger bowls with scented rose petals came with them. We savoured every minute of eating at a table laid with a clean white cloth, enjoying a whole rare steak which had not been chopped into little pieces. Fresh strawberries and a lot of French wine left us feeling ready for anything.

8

HORSE-COPING IN NORTHERN SHAANXI

T he drive to northern Shaanxi took three days. We were all in high spirits at being off again. Mr Li, who had taken the brunt of our impatience at the delay, said, 'This lightens my mental burden considerably.'

We left Xian through a fine gateway in the massive walls and plunged at once into a ghastly industrial suburb. I found my mood, my whole attitude towards China often changed as swiftly, so that I sometimes alternated between awestruck admiration and outright disgust. Their past and present attainments are outstanding. The level of culture reached repeatedly during successive dynasties was so superior and produced so many exquisite objects. Life at court must have represented at many times civilization of a very high order during eras when most of the rest of the world was producing nothing remotely comparable. But we are told, and unquestionably it was true much of the time, that, like many empires, it was based on great cruelty, slavery and the oppression of the vast majority of the people.

Today I am constantly amazed by China's very real success story. The country now works as an entity and it is clearly on its way for the first time ever along lines broadly acceptable to the masses and which they have no great desire to change. Nearly everyone looks happy and reasonably well fed; there is a dynamism and an enthusiasm in the air which one can practically feel. Crops grow, factories produce, there is next to no unemployment and all is rush and hustle. Perhaps the most impressive aspect of all this is that it is not being attempted too fast. Some of the best from the West is being taken without it being allowed to contaminate, as seems to happen all too often elsewhere. This is because the Chinese refuse to allow experts from abroad to come and do whatever needs to be done efficiently and quickly, but instead insist, often to the hair-tearing fury of foreign joint-venture partners, on doing it in a slow and experimental, essentially Chinese way, which allows them to learn from their mistakes. This seems to me a wise policy, provided irreplaceable treasures like the terracotta army are not put at risk in the process.

But progress has been bought at a heavy price and I have to question whether it has been worth it. After leading the world for so long in cultural principles and achievements, China today appears to have lost its soul and with it all aesthetic sense. Everywhere we looked the buildings were not just utilitarian, which was understandable in a poor developing country, but they were hideous, badly furnished and appallingly maintained. With the exception of a couple of modern hotels and office blocks we barely saw a large building in China which had not at least one broken window pane, some of the roof falling off or streaks of dirt down the walls. Inside, the decor was always atrocious, lacking the faintest colour or design sense and nothing was ever properly finished. Carpets curled at the corners, stains were not removed, pipes were exposed and leaked. Even in clothes, where there has been a rapid revolution in the last few years from the dull conformity of blue tunics to a great freedom of dress, especially among the young, there seemed to be very little taste, style or sense of fashion. These are not criticisms which can be excused on the grounds that the country is poor or that it is preoccupied with progress rather than taste. India is a much poorer country but grace and beauty shine among the squalor. Malaysia and Indonesia have many poor regions where life is not dissimilar to that of the mainland Chinese. Yet there the women are elegant, buildings are cared for and there is a sense of quality. I suppose the difference has to be the political system and perhaps the same could be said of any communist country. But it seems such a pity that a political philosophy which is justly credited with having removed the oppression and regular famine suffered previously should have to have such a disastrous effect on the finer things of life. I hope I am wrong. The fact that in the cities people flock to concerts by visiting western musicians indicates that I may be and there were a great many areas of China's cultural life of which I saw nothing. The desire to learn is there and in due course a new, cultured generation may emerge. It may be unfair, but in the end history remembers and admires eras and dynasties more for producing pyramids, poetry, paintings and porcelain than cement, coal, cars and cuckoo clocks. Man cannot, and should not, try to live by rice alone.

Driving in China is always an interesting experience, but our journey back up to the Great Wall was exceptional. Mr Bo was an excellent, fast and quite aggressive driver, a necessity in a country where no quarter is given to the weak. The problem, as my Aunt Madge used to say, was the other damn fools on the road. Louella and I had chosen to sit in the front of our minibus, next to Mr Bo, so as to see as much as possible. This meant that there was nothing in front of us except the large glass windscreen. It was good for taking photographs but fatal for us if we hit anything since seatbelts were unknown in China. There were no cars on the road, just an endless procession of

Driving in China is always an interesting experience, especially in loess country, where rivers have cut deep ravines and roads have collapsed.

lorries driven by maniacs. When heavily loaded with coal or rocks and dragging equally heavy trailers behind them, they spewed acrid black smoke and swayed dangerously from side to side. When empty they drove flat out, overtaking on blind corners, bouncing wildly in and out of ruts and potholes, and blowing their air horns constantly. This was the only part of our journey when we were in real and constant danger of death.

After we left the outskirts of Xian we passed through beautiful farming country where the harvest was being gathered amid scenes of bucolic contentment. For a time these alternated with towns which were archetypes of industrial pollution: terrible dark satanic mills surrounded by slums, where factory chimneys discharged clouds of pitch black or sinister white smoke, which fell on the road and caused noxious dust. In between the towns the landscape became more and more lovely, making another Chinese contrast. This was loess country. Loess is fine yellowish soil, probably the dust of northern Asia which has been blown down into China for thousands of years and now covers the land to a depth of hundreds of feet. Another theory is that it is the primeval mud from the bottom of an ancient sea, which once covered this land. Once it was forested, but now it has been stripped. Rivers have cut deep ravines through the loess and as a result the landscape, which appears to consist simply of a series of great beige plains and softly contoured hills, is actually full of sudden sheer valleys at the bottom of which lush bushes and trees crowd the narrow stream beds. The soil can be quite fertile where it is possible to cultivate and irrigate it, and almost everywhere we saw evidence of efforts to do so. Terracing continued right up to the edge of terrifying brown cliffs and we could see distant figures of men and donkeys ploughing within feet of vertical drops.

Some of the hills were covered in a white flowering shrub and the acacia, too, was in bloom. All along the road migrant beekeepers were out in force, living in tents beside their rows of hives. A few wore hats and veils, especially when working on the hives, but most sat quietly smoking pipes and whittling pieces of wood. We saw no honey for sale. Perhaps it was too early in the year.

At Huangling, where we spent the first night, there was a hotel, but we skipped dinner and instead climbed through cobbled streets up to the wooded hill above the town. Huang, the Yellow Emperor, is the legendary father of the Chinese people and is said to have lived 5,000 years ago. He has always been revered as the inventor of almost everything useful and important to China, such as the making of silk from silkworms, weaving, writing, the wheel and the compass. Travellers passing his tomb used to have to dismount from their horses and pay their respects to their First Ancestor. Today it is guarded by a surrounding wall and a great many lovely old twisted cypress trees. There are supposed to be 63,000 of them, one having been planted by the Emperor himself. We strolled peacefully in the cool shade of the wood, passing an elderly shepherd watching over a herd of cows with bells round their necks. There were burial mounds and a stela bearing three gilded characters. It was a wonderfully tranquil place of magic glades from which we glimpsed inspiring views through the trees of terraced hillsides far away. As Louella said, it felt quite unlike China, more like the background of a Renaissance painting.

As we approached Yanan conventional houses became rare and almost everyone lived in caves. In the loess this made good sense, especially as the winters are bitterly cold and the summers very hot. Presumably loess cannot easily be made into bricks. Instead rooms the shape of small Nissen huts are dug into the side of the hills, the fronts are bricked up, a door and window are built in, and a chimney is poked up to emerge through the soil above. Two or three of these rooms side by side make a good house, well insulated and relatively easy, quick and cheap to build. They reminded us very much of the shelters underneath the arches below London railway lines. Sometimes they interconnect, but usually a family will build a yard around its particular row of doors. Some had a short stretch of quite grand castellation along the top of the front or intricate trellis work around the door and

(*above*) In northern Shaanxi, three million people live in caves.

(*below*) Houses are dug into the sides of the loess hills. They are warm in winter and cool in summer.

window. The 'railway cuttings' design was, we found, incorporated into some of the modern buildings in Yanan and we also saw several modern cave 'condominiums' outside the town: two or three tiered rows of caves clearly built as a municipal effort. Cave dwelling really must be practical in that region and it was the standard form of habitation.

Yanan is a famous place in Chinese communist mythology as it was Mao's headquarters after the 'Long March'. The cave he lived in is preserved and there are museums visited by the Party faithful much as their parents visited famous temples on pilgrimages. The rest of the town is an ugly sprawl of factories squeezed in a narrow canyon along the Yan river into which all the town's effluent flows. Only a fine nine-storey Song Dynasty pagoda on a cliff gives the place character. To the north the loess continued and the road deteriorated. We drove along river beds, along narrow ledges and up winding hairpin corniches to plateaus, where many of the cave villages had been abandoned.

It was a windswept, wild region, the loess carved into extraordinary patterns and designs by man and nature. The water-eroded canyons were rugged, the man-made terraces smooth and regular like contour lines on a map.

The Long March ended at a place called Wuqi in October 1935. During the previous year well over a hundred thousand people had died as the Red Army fought its way 6,000 miles across China. Only seven or eight thousand ragged survivors had staggered into Wuqi, then a village of only seven families. We stopped there to find a rather ugly town of about 4,000 people on the edge of a muddy river. While our crew went off to see if they could find a restaurant for lunch we were told not to leave our bus. 'You must not get down. This is a closed area,' said Mr Li. They returned having failed to find anywhere to eat. 'This place is not clean,' they said. It was only much later that we learned of the special position it holds in modern Chinese history.

The land became progressively poorer and drier until at last we emerged on the third day of driving to see a hazy plain stretching away northwards; and quite clearly the Great Wall again marked the boundary of cultivation. Here it was a very different Wall to that in Hebei province. The original scale and design must have been broadly similar, but because there was little or no stone here, the Wall was made of mud and much of it had melted away over the centuries. Once again it was the watch towers which stood out, now shapeless lumps of pitted adobe. Between them often only a mound, like a low ridge, marked where the Wall had once been. As we drove down on to the plain there were trees planted along the roadside and mules pulling carts. We looked out for horses, but saw none. 'You can't have mules without horses,' I said optimistically.

Our crew near Wuqi where the Long March ended: Mr Li the interpreter, Mr He the cook and Mr Bo the driver.

At Dingbian the 'relevant authorities' were supposed to have been warned about our arrival and our pressing need to find some horses on which to continue our ride. They had heard nothing and we had to start from scratch. However, they were friendly and willing, though pessimistic, as they said that mechanization was making horses scarce nowadays. We were taken back eastwards along the Wall to a village called Zhengjingbu where we were told there was a horse market. All the way on the 18 mile (30 kilometre) drive we could see the Wall temptingly on our left; stretches of the ramparts were visible, not just blank spaces between the ruined towers. It was a huge relief to see that it really did exist here, too, and that there should be no great difficulty in following it. Beyond there was desert, real sand dune desert stretching as far as the eye could see. It looked frightening and uncrossable. Although I knew from the maps I had studied that the Mu Us desert lay beyond the Wall here, I had not realized that the sand would come right up to and even over it in places. That was Mongolia out there, the Autonomous Region of Inner Mongolia, which we had no permission to visit. The invaders from the north must have been hard men, we thought, and so must those who live there today.

The village was quite small, just one dusty street between single-storey mud houses, and it lay right against a massive crumbling fort where a garrison must have once been housed. As soon as we stepped down from our bus, we were surrounded by a jostling, staring crowd of all ages, the teenage boys pushing their way to the front. Mr Li volunteered the information that we were the first foreigners they had ever seen, this being a closed area. We all walked through to the market, a wide sandy space enclosed by a mud wall. There were several mules and donkeys but at first no sign of a horse. Then a very small, thin chestnut gelding of barely 12 hands was led up. It appeared most unpromising, but I had a look at its teeth, which were long in front, implying considerable age, but clean and white under the muck it was chewing lugubriously. I suggested that it was very old and its owner assured us it was five. On my expressing doubt this was amended to eight, but there was no trace of a cuspid hook and my doubts remained. It looked a hundred, but when its owner leapt on to it bareback and careered around among the crowd it seemed quite willing to oblige and appeared to have a nice nature.

The crowd were very pressing and so we retired to the relative peace of our bus, where they came and pressed their noses to the windows. A splendid farouche character, the local horse coper, now joined us as well as a couple of 'local authorities' to see fair play. The coper said he would send for some good horses, which would be there by the evening. 'Melon patch and plum tree!' said Louella. This was a nice expression we had come across in our Chinese phrase book indicating suspicion. Often in Chinese four single characters are used to express quite a complicated piece of imagery. In this case the words were a shortened version of 'when walking in a melon field don't stop to adjust your shoes, when walking under plum trees don't reach up to straighten your cap', meaning that if you do so people will think you are stealing melons or plums. We found it a delightful form of shorthand, which helped to prevent us getting irritated whenever we suspected we were being manipulated. There was seldom much else we could do about it.

The authorities kindly offered us the use of their office in which to sit out the day, but we drove back to Dingbian instead. There we unpacked all our riding gear, spread it out in a rather smelly open area next to the public latrine and gave it a thorough going over with our precious leather dressing. As always a crowd gathered to watch in silent incredulity at first as we worked away. When they began to chatter and laugh we asked Mr Li what they were saying about us. 'Oh, just that foreigners are not so very different after all except for the colour of their hair and the shape of their eyes.' Once again I felt that the fact we were doing something so familiar and normal as to rub down and repair leather saddles and bridles made us seem less alien and different than other tourists. These, with the freedom unknown in China to travel where they wished, able to spend a year's Chinese income in a day, hurrying through the eternal landscape in air conditioned limousines, must seem very strange indeed.

A young English teacher from the local school called Mr Ma, which means horse, emerged from the crowd and in quite good English asked

A sea of interested faces gathered around us whenever we stopped in a village.

if we would come and talk to his class. We promised to do so if we were not able to leave at dawn next day, as we hoped to do. Mr He was back in his element singing cheerfully as he cooked supper for us after an interlude during which he had become silent and withdrawn, feeling useless.

Back at Zhengjingbu an even bigger and more eager crowd had gathered to see the fun. After the delays in Xian we were desperate to be off and had decided we would take anything we were offered just so that we could be in the saddle again and doing what we had come to China for. The coper arrived with the two fine specimens he had promised to procure for us. One was a slightly larger chestnut than the one we had seen in the morning, about 13 hands. It had an ugly cropped mane and a nasty skin disease which made its head and neck scabrous and its head was mulish and plain. But it had good legs, neat feet, younger teeth and its ribs hardly showed at all. I put my saddle on it and managed to persuade it to canter up and down the village street while the crowd gaped, clapped, and parted like the Red Sea. We agreed that it would have to do for me as there seemed no prospect of doing any better. The second horse, which Louella tried out, was a little black foal. The coper assured us it was four years old, but it had the feathery tail of a foal, little spindly legs and it nearly fell over when she put her saddle on it. We told him it would not do and asked if he could get us another. This, it seemed, might be possible but would involve a day or two of waiting while the surrounding countryside was scoured. 'Are there no other horses here?' we asked. 'None,' he replied. At that moment a cart trundled past with an old man asleep in the back. Between the shafts was the chestnut horse of the morning. 'We'll have that one,' we said in unison, and soon Louella was mounted on it and succeeded in urging it into a reluctant canter.

The discussion about price now began. Horse dealing is the same all over the world. It is a matter of character, humour and bluff as much as a business transaction. Mr Li now showed an unexpected and admirable side of his nature by entering into the spirit of the negotiations with the enthusiasm of an old hand. He and the old rogue of a coper began to nudge each other in the ribs, and exchange secret signals by putting their hands inside each other's clothes and extending fingers to indicate different amounts. I was suddenly transported back to the Irish village fairs of my youth, where much the same sort of knowing nudging and winking would accompany a deal. There, it is true, many visits to the pub would also be obligatory in order to close the matter, but the general atmosphere was familiar. The coper was wearing a straw hat like a solar topee, an old cardigan and extraordi-

Louella trying out the most unpromising pony on which she eventually rode another four hundred miles.

The horse coper of Zhengjingbu from whom we bought Yang and Yin.

narily old fashioned dark glasses. Mr Li was, as always, in a spotless white shirt and he, of course, had to refer to us from time to time to see how far he could go.

We settled at 750 yuan for my horse and 600 yuan for Louella's. This represented about £150 and £120 respectively. It was, we suspected, a good bit more than the local market price but any horse dealer worth his salt knows when he has the opposition over a barrel and our protagonist had, as we were well aware, seen us coming from a long way off. When the deal was concluded Mr Li told us proudly that the coper had made a special price for us because of the signi-ficance of what we were doing. 'He was working for the dignity and honour of his country when he sold us those horses,' he said. The chances of dignity and honour alone getting us safely over the next three or four hundred miles seemed slim to us as we looked at the wretched creatures we had been landed with. We decided to call them Yang and Yin after the two forces which maintain harmony in the universe.

As we walked our new mounts up and down we could see the coper counting out our money and then standing heroically in the doorway of our bus holding the wad of notes above his head. He looked ominously like Fagin as he beamed around.

9

INTO THE PLAINS OF NINGXIA

T o our surprise, everything was ready early in the morning and we were away for the start of stage two of our journey by 8 a.m. The whole village saw us off, hemming us in, feeling our saddles and our leather chaps. Yang and Yin were very good and tripped along merrily. Yang had a rather faster pace and Louella had to urge Yin to catch up from time to time but he did so fairly readily. He had a pretty head with a sweet expression and round his neck was a cord from which hung a small brass bell with no clapper. He was very thin and his feet were a mess. We had asked Mr Li to try and find a blacksmith to shoe both horses that evening if possible.

I had hoped we would have been able to find better mounts as we were not far from the borders of both Mongolia and Ningxia, regions once celebrated for their horses. The only previous foreigner I knew who had travelled anywhere near where we now were was Edgar Snow, the American who went on the Long March with Mao. In 1936 he had been only a few miles away with the First Red Cavalry, which he described as the pride of the army. They were mounted, he says, 'on about 3,000 beautiful Ninghsia [Wade-Giles] ponies, fine fleet animals taller and stronger than the Mongolian ponies of North China, with sleek flanks and well-filled buttocks.' Anything less like Yin would be hard to imagine. He was lent 'a splendid Ninghsia pony, strong as a bull, that gave me one of the wildest rides of my life . . . The trouble with that ride was the wooden Chinese saddle, so narrow that I could not sit in the seat, but had to ride on my inner thighs the whole distance, while the short, heavy iron stirrups cramped my legs'.

At least we had our own deep and comfortable saddles, which made riding almost any horse a pleasure. Cantering on them was glorious, like rolling along in an armchair, but it was hard to make our new mounts keep it up for more than a few minutes at a time before they dropped back into a slow amble, the sort of gait used for pulling a cart. Not so Edgar Snow's pony. 'The road lay level across the plain for over fifty li [17 miles (27 kilometres)]. In that whole distance we got down to a walk just once. We raced at a steady gallop for the last five miles, and at the finish swept up the main street of Yu Wang Pao with my companions trailing far behind. Before P'eng's headquarters I slithered off and examined my mount, expecting him to topple over in a faint. He was puffing very slightly and had a few beads of sweat on him, but was otherwise quite unruffled, the beast.'

We rode north of Zhengjingbu along a sandy lane between old mud-walled houses until we came to the remains of a great fortress. A fine stretch of Wall with arches still remaining in places surrounded a patch of cultivation. The track passed through what must have once been a grand gateway but had by now completely vanished and at once we were in wonderful country outside. On either side the Wall stretched away to the horizon while ahead lay the great Mu Us desert. We turned west and followed a level sandy track beside the remains of the Wall. There was no mistaking the substantial mound which marked where it had once been and following it all the way through the part we had been forced to circumvent would not, it seemed, have been at all difficult. It was much eroded, with sand blown up against it, but the continuous low hummock crested at times to make a ridge one could not ride over and most of the regular watch towers were still there as squared off lumps of mud 20 or 30 feet (6 or 9 metres) high.

It was pleasantly cool, a nice hazy day and we kept saying to each other, 'Isn't this perfection?' The ground was carpeted with wild flowers, which I stopped to photograph from time to time thinking they might be rare. Yang stood still as soon as I dismounted. I thought how well trained he must be and stopped bothering to hold his reins, as

The author by a cutting through the remains of the Wall, now only a continuous low hummock.

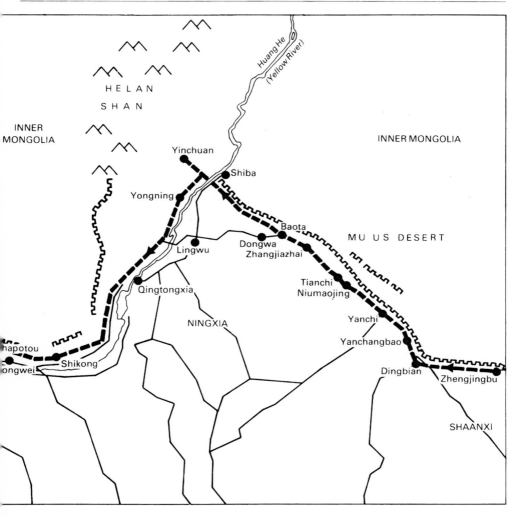

The western end of the Wall.

this left my hands free for the camera. There were yellow blooms like
cowslips, purple convolvulus and another creeping plant like a clover
as well as lots of smaller white flowers. Pale fawn lizards about five
inches long with pointed tails scurried away from the horses' feet and
there were butterflies everywhere. Sometimes whole clouds of white
ones enveloped us. There were yellow ones, among which I saw some
swallow-tails, and some very pretty tiny blues. With larks overhead,
flocks of sparrows chirping as they raided the crops and white, presumably tame, doves flying past us to perch on the Wall, it was all quite
magical and I felt a premonition that such perfection could not last.

For some hours we rode along on top of the remains of the Wall
itself. This gave us a good view out over the sand dunes to the north,

where we could see salt flats shining white, and across the plain to the south backed by the high yellow mountains of loess. We put up a large hare with a black spot on the tip of its tail, which lolloped absent-mindedly away from us, not in the least afraid. There were lots of small holes in the ground, which we had to watch out the horses did not step in. They were made by small stout rodents which sat up to whistle at us before diving into them. I took them to be marmots, but they may have been pikas. We also saw a dead hedgehog on a rubbish heap outside a cave house built into the Wall itself. These dwellings tended to be on the inner side of the Wall so that riding along the outside and on top often all we saw of them as we passed was a stovepipe chimney incongruously sticking up out of the ground. The soil looked unprom-isingly poor and the crops, where they were being attempted, were thin. But the occasional people we saw working on the land were friendly and waved to us as we rode by. We stopped to photograph a little girl and her smaller brother whom we had surprised as we rode around a section of mud Wall. She stood her ground bravely, her eyes wide with amazement at the sight of us, but the little boy ran off screaming hysterically as though we were about to kill him. Fortu-nately their parents were nearby, ploughing behind a couple of donkeys. They laughed, seeing that we meant no harm, and we gave them one of our explanatory handouts to pore over.

Later, as we approached Dingbian, we came to slightly more fertile soil, where the land was divided up by long straight double rows of poplars and willows, which presumably marked out the boundaries between different communes as well as creating windbreaks. They made lovely shady glades to canter along, grassy underfoot and cooler than being out on the plain.

We had arranged to meet our crew at an exceptionally large fort, which could be seen from the road some way out of Dingbian. We arrived there before them in the early afternoon and looked forward to a good rest to stretch our limbs. I tied my reins up so that Yang could graze and suggested to Louella that she should do the same with Yin. She was doubtful about letting him go, but I assured her that it was quite safe as they were both tired and Yang had proved that he had no desire to escape. As I took a photograph of the horses and Louella in front of the fort, she hesitated, wondering if it would not be sensible to hold on to Yin. Once released, he began to wander over towards Yang and we both thought better of it and decided to tie them up. But as we walked towards them they looked at us, then at each other and, before we could move or speak, took off at high speed. 'It's all right,' I said through gritted teeth, 'They'll stop in a minute and carry on grazing.' But they failed to do so and we looked on helplessly as they galloped back the way we had come, their stirrups flapping and their heels kicking in the air as they disappeared over the horizon. I have seldom

A cave house built into the Wall itself. Here it was made of mud and much of it had melted away, leaving only crumbling watch towers.

felt more foolish or more furious with myself. All the magic of the day evaporated and I cursed ceaselessly for several minutes. Louella waited patiently for me to finish and then we set off in pursuit, trudging glumly along through the soft sand in our riding boots.

As we passed a farm several large and angry dogs rushed out barking. We felt defenceless on foot but managed, by walking determinedly on, to avoid being attacked. At the same time a dust storm hit us. It was not particularly severe but the warm, thick swirling cloud depressed us further as we plodded on.

At last we met our bus and crew back on the road and soon after Mr He spotted a group of people in the distance. They were holding a horse, which proved to be Yang. Saddle and bridle were undamaged and he seemed fresh as a daisy. Filled with renewed energy, I thanked them and leapt on, galloping off in the direction they said Yin had gone. Thundering back down one of the long glades of trees on the assumption Yin was still heading for home, I came on one of the friendly farmers who had waved as we passed. 'Ni kan ma ma? [have you seen a horse?],' I asked, rather pleased with myself at being able to construct a useful phrase at need. I also mimed and mumbled my way through an explanation of what had happened. He got the message right away and quite clearly told me that the only horses he had seen all day had been ours riding the other way.

A kiln near Dingbian where the remains of the Wall are being made into bricks.

I cast about among the windbreaks and after half an hour or so Louella, now riding Yin and accompanied by a boy riding bareback, found me. It seemed that an old man, who had watched us go by during the morning, had seen our riderless animals gallop back again. 'Those must belong to the Foreign Guests,' he had said. 'You, Number Two Son, must go and catch them for them,' and he had done so. We were, of course, very grateful, took Polaroid pictures of all the family and pressed them to accept a reward, which they tried hard to refuse. 'There is no need to be grateful,' they said to Mr Li. 'It is the duty of every Chinese person to help Foreign Guests.' We were so touched as well as being relieved to have back the horses, who seemed to have done themselves no damage, that all our good humour was restored.

Having added a good nine miles to our day's ride, we continued into Dingbian, where Mr Li had arranged lodging for the horses in the courtyard of a delightful extended family. Elderly grandparents presided over a number of married sons and daughters and several small babies. The horses were tied to a pile of logs and we were taken indoors to be fed on hot orange juice, made from crystals, and glutinous rice which we dipped into a bowl of sugar. It was just what we needed as we waited for the blacksmith to arrive.

He was old and grizzled, irritable and stone deaf but clearly a considerable local character. He had with him a string of improbably shaped iron shoes tied in a bundle and some very primitive tools. There was no question of a forge, but he hammered away until the front two more or less fitted each horse and then he banged them on cold with his home made nails. He refused to touch the hind feet, even to trim them, and I could see daylight in places between shoe and hoof in the front, but he assured us they would stay on for 1,000 miles. Everyone said he was a wonderful blacksmith, who had shod the horses of Marshall Peng Dehuai, one of the greatest heroes of the Long March. This was the same Peng mentioned by Edgar Snow and it was good to have even such a tenuous link with him; he sounded one of the more attractive characters from that time.

Edgar Snow describes him as 'a gay, laughter-loving man, in excellent health . . . physically very active, an excellent rider, and a man of endurance'. He loved children and was followed by a group of young delinquents who had run away from home to join the Red Army and whom he called his 'little Red devils'. He was a brilliant guerilla fighter against the Japanese, coining the phrase 'the people are the sea, while the guerillas are the fish swimming in it' and in the Korean War he led the 400,000 'Chinese People's Volunteers' against the Americans, forcing them back across the 38th parallel and capturing Seoul.

Later he was to be Mao's Defence Minister and one of the most powerful and respected revolutionary leaders. But after the disastrous Great Leap Forward in 1959 he dared to criticize Mao, blaming him quite rightly for the chaos and calling it 'petty bourgeois fanaticism'. He lost the subsequent political battle and was replaced by Lin Biao. For his temerity he was humiliated and beaten by Red Guards during the Cultural Revolution. He died in 1974 without being reinstated. Ironically, the only English book Chinese students were ever allowed to read during the terrible Eleven Years was *Red Star Over China*, but that version was abridged to remove the passages mentioning Peng Dehuai, whom Edgar Snow had admired so much.

We managed to leave Dingbian before dawn next morning, before the strident lady on the loudspeakers all over town roused the workers with inspiring slogans. We had spent much of the night packing and sorting our gear, and preparing our supplies, since we were about to head out into country where, we were told, we were unlikely to find anything. We were pretty sure Mr He would always manage to find food in local markets, but we had to be ready to come up with meals from our packaged resources if necessary.

It was extremely good to be on our way at first light again. The family were only rubbing the sleep out of their eyes as we rode out of their courtyard, cocks were crowing and the sun was catching the top of the town wall. The Great Wall makes a right angle turn to the north at Dingbian and we managed to get a bit confused and lost trying to ride around the outskirts of the town instead of through the middle. At last we picked up the Wall again and were once more able to ride along

The Wall leaving the grassland to disappear into the Mu Us Desert.

a very broken stretch across a grassy plain until we crossed the road. Here we had to make a decision. Ahead the Wall disappeared into the dramatic sand dunes of the Mu Us desert. It seemed mad to head into such patently inhospitable country when there was an alternative. To our left the road made a wide dog leg to the west; that would be safe, easy to follow, and rather dull. We decided to risk it, cantered across the last mile or so of grass, and rode up across the sand into the dunes. It was like being transported into the heart of the Sahara, though we felt more as though we were acting parts in a Western as we dismounted to lead our horses up the steeper slopes. The sand was surprisingly stable and once we stopped worrying about quicksands we began to enjoy ourselves and make good time. There were no other tracks of man or beast and it was quite frightening being, as it were, out of sight of land. But with the remains of the Wall running straight and true through the shifting sand hills, we were unlikely to get lost. It was not even too hot to begin with and right out in the middle we came on a pool of clear water from which both horses drank.

At the highest point in the dunes, a spot marked as being 4,648 feet (1416 metres) on my US Airforce map, we saw ahead the remains of a large square fort commanding a fantastic view in all directions. To our surprise there seemed to be a house built in it. At this point we were able to ride along the actual top of the Wall and so we made a dramatic arrival at this remarkably isolated place. An old man was hoeing an unpromising piece of sandy garden nearby. He stopped work and

Far out in the desert there were no tracks, but it was impossible to get lost while we could see traces of the Wall.

'In the middle we came on a pool of clear water from which both the horses drank.'

came up into the fort to talk to us. The house proved to be a simple little square temple. We dismounted and entered, to be astounded by a large poster of a richly dressed man on a fine white horse. We assumed it was the Emperor Qin on the horse which, legend has it, showed the builders where to build the Wall, but what an unlikely place to come across it!

Next to it was a small brass Buddha and incense sticks had been burned below in a carved stone container. The old man, when he saw our interest, reverently brought out two more Buddhas which were wrapped in cloth. One was bronze and looked old. He also produced a

At the highest point in the dunes, as we were riding along the top of the mound beneath which the Wall was buried, we came on the remains of a large fort where a small house had been built.

box of incense sticks, some matches and a candle. We each lit a stick from the candle, salaamed reverently to the Buddha and stood for a moment peacefully together as the scented smoke curled upwards. It was a totally unexpected moment of sheer enchantment. The old man must have been a monk who had escaped persecution and chosen to live far from the rest of mankind.

Next to the temple was a cosy cave house dug into the wall of the fort and beside it a pen for his animals. There were chickens and a family of large white rabbits, which had just had a litter of tiny fluffy white babies. To complete the magic for me there were four choughs nesting in holes in the wall above. A tranquil place, miles from anywhere, on top of the world. He cordially invited us to stay and sup with him, but we thanked him and declined.

As we crossed the border between Shaanxi and Ningxia we could see another Wall far to the north. This one was also marked on the map, one of the many stretches which add up to give the ridiculous quoted lengths of the Great Wall. Official Chinese sources go as high as 3,700 miles, or 6,000 kilometres and more which, if they referred to one continuous Wall, would take it virtually to Moscow. Here, too, we saw big salt lakes with piles of white salt being extracted.

Yanchi was the first town in Ningxia and as we rode in we found that Yang had cast one of his shoes and was going quite lame. We walked up the main street with me leading Yang and the inevitable crowd gathered around us. It was stiflingly hot, the crowd hemmed us in leaving no air so that we felt claustrophobic, and it was depressing being unable to continue. We needed another blacksmith and it took an age to find one, while we waited with the horses tied to a telegraph pole. Beside us was the town bank and after a time the manager came out and kindly invited us in to rest, offering his premises as a haven from the crowd. We accepted gratefully and found it much cooler inside, sitting on the long wooden counter. Unfortunately the populace followed us in and soon the crush and heat were as bad as before. The manager was a gentle soul and so in the end I had to push them all out with the help of the cleaner and then bar the door against them. Business was now totally interrupted but no one seemed to mind. Instead the three female bank staff, who all had babies with them and appeared to be the manager's daughters and nieces, giggled over pictures of our children with Louella and in return allowed her to cuddle their babies one by one.

At last Yang's problem was sorted out and we were able to be on our way again. Now we were riding along beside a road. Since most of the traffic was four legged there was a good soft verge and we could always cut across the open plain when the road curved. It was exactly what we had expected Ningxia to be like; a wide open country of shepherds grazing their flocks on poor grass growing on sandy soil. It was perfect riding country and there were even trees planted on either side of the road to give a dappled shade.

As we cantered merrily along a lorry approached, the driver as always tooting his horn and leaning out of the window to stare at us. He shouted the Chinese equivalent of 'ride him, cowboy!' while his companion whistled and ogled from his side. Seconds after they passed there was a loud bang and we looked back to see that the driver had been so captivated by the sight of us that he had driven straight into a tree. It was a large tree, which the lorry had snapped in half, at the same time shedding its load of crates and bottles.

We had been hoping for a long time that some kind of poetic justice would punish one of the more outrageous gapers, but we had only thought in terms of bicyclists. This was beyond our greatest expectations. No one was hurt, but the mess was appalling and the loss of face acute. We snatched a couple of photographs and cantered away. Being in China we were likely to be blamed for the accident if we lingered and we were rather ashamed of having such strong feelings of schadenfreude.

We stayed in a good mood for the rest of the afternoon, waving to shepherds as we passed, the only figures in the wide, rolling landscape except for occasional beekeepers. It was evening as we came to the hamlet of Niumaojing, where we planned to spend the night. At the first mud house two large yellow dogs, like Alsatians, rushed out savagely and leapt up at Louella. Fortunately she was carrying a stick and was able to beat them off, but without it she would almost certainly have been bitten.

Our crew had arranged an excellent camp site, a roadmenders' compound which was clean, with a deep well from which pure cold water was drawn for us and for the horses. They had a sandy enclosure under some trees and plenty of chopped straw as well as their maize and black beans. We had been unable to obtain bran and they seemed content, if rather prone to wind, on this diet.

Writing up my diary that evening I realized that it was 4 June, a day of special significance to Etonians for a reason I am not alone in forgetting. One of the books we had with us was Peter Fleming's classic, my favourite travel book about China, *News from Tartary*. He and Ella Maillart made their epic journey under infinitely more arduous conditions than we experienced and over a far greater distance, but they must have been among the last foreigners to ride any distance across China before us and we felt a modest link with them for that. I turned to the passage where Peter Fleming describes the day exactly fifty-one years before, when they were about 1,000 miles to the west in Sinkiang:

We camped in a little pass beside a stream, on what would soon be turf. It was a pleasant place, and here we celebrated no less an anniversary than the Fourth of June; its significance, I fear, was rather lost on Kini, for my attempts to explain the connection between George III and fireworks at Eton were handicapped by the regrettable discovery that I had really no idea what the connection was; moreover, William Tell somehow got into the conversation and confused the issue badly. Still, we made a light but sybaritic lunch off a very small tin of crab which had been given me, seven months before, by the Japanese Consul-General in Vladivostock and which I had been carrying about Asia as a kind of talisman ever since. We amused ourselves by trying to imagine how one would set about explaining what a crab was to the Turkis, who had never heard of the sea and lived 2,000 miles from the nearest bit of it.

In the evening I climbed a shoulder above the pass and did an abortive stalk after some antelope. The sun had gone and the great uplands had a very desolate air. But I felt gay and light-headed, and full of a conviction that I was invincible, that nothing was going to stop me from getting through to India. But even in this braggart mood, when success seemed so well worth achieving, I knew in my heart how sadly little the feat would be worth in retrospect — how easy it would all prove to have been, how many opportunities one would curse oneself for having missed. One's *alter ego* is at times an irritating companion.

Mine was powerless, however, to qualify the delights of the whacking great meal which we ate that evening in honour of the Fourth of June. We got out the brandy and the gramophone and played our three records several times and our favourite record over and over again; it was a saccharine and cretinous ditty called 'The Clouds Will Soon Roll By' which Kini had taken, when she first saw the title, for a musical fantasia on a meteorological theme. I can hear it now . . .

> Somewhere a robin's singing,
>   Up in a tree-top high;
> To you and me he's singing,
>   'The clouds will soon roll by.'

It was a most reassuring kind of song.

We had no brandy or gramophone, but we had Mr He's delectable dumplings with which to celebrate. Afterwards we went for a starlit walk out into the desert beyond the walls of our compound. The cluster of flat-roofed mud houses lay in the centre of a great bowl of space with a horizon that stretched right round; it was like being at sea. A single tree was silhouetted against the paler western sky and there was absolute peace and quiet. It was cool and serene under the stars, all was well and we had a comfortable mattress and warm sleeping bags waiting for us, lit by the romantic glow of a kerosene lamp. We felt no braggart mood, just a sense of great contentment that we were achieving what we had set out to do.

10

BETWEEN THE DESERT AND THE GREEN

T he tranquillity of awakening to a cool clear morning with no loudspeaker sent us off in a happy mood. The roadworkers were friendly and proud to have entertained us, though in truth it was we who had entertained them with our strange ways. The high point of our performance had been when I pumped up our inflatable mattress. The pump squeaked regularly and attracted the whole community of a dozen or so, who watched entranced and speculated on what on earth it could be for. Laid on a concrete floor it made all the difference between sound sleep and aching bones and we found it well worth the effort. Using it reminded us of the immortal last paragraph of Eric Newby's *A Short Walk in the Hindu Kush*, the funniest of modern travel books. After suffering appalling hardships in Nuristan, the heroes of the story met the legendary Wilfred Thesiger and made camp with him. ' "Let's turn in," he said. The ground was like iron with sharp rocks sticking up out of it. We started to blow up our air-beds. "God, you must be a couple of pansies," said Thesiger.'

We cantered away waving farewell and promising to return. Our route was unmistakable as we were between the only road and the Wall, both of which stretched away to the northwest as far as the eye could see. A dangerous euphoria overcame us as we sped hand in hand over the perfect surface of gently undulating grassland. We imagined conversations we would have on our return to England, when we would tell our friends that the only decent place left in the world for riding now was Ningxia and they really must go there for a holiday. We felt confident that nothing could now go wrong. Of course it immediately did.

As we were at our most ecstatic and irresponsible, urging our horses faster, side by side we plunged into an invisible quicksand. Louella was pitched right over Yin's head and my first ungallant thought was to regret that I did not have my camera at the ready. Then we were both too busy struggling to beat and drag the horses clear before they sank in too deeply to be able to scramble out. The morass was caused by water from an apparently dry streambed, which had seeped under the

Cantering happily across the Ningxia plain towards the hidden quicksands.

sand to create a trap. Fortunately the surrounding land was firm and we were soon safe, but both Louella, who had knocked her ankle, and Yin were lame for some time and we all walked until we got our nerve back.

It was a day of following the long straight empty road across featureless country, enlivened only by a series of quite unpleasant dust storms. Fortunately the wind was from the east and so in our backs, which made things more bearable, but the grit swirled into our eyes, noses and mouths, making our teeth grate, while the surface of the ground was a constantly shifting film of eddying windblown sand and dust. There was a kind of tumbleweed, too, which blew past us, adding to the sense of desolation. In spite of the poor visibility in the storms, when it was like being in a thick fog, we were never in danger of being lost as there were almost always rows of poplars planted along both sides of the road. In spite of the barrenness of the region, and although they bent in the wind, these trees seemed to be surviving, a hopeful sign of change and the only possible protection against the constantly encroaching sand.

In between the storms we could see that the ground was carpeted in places with pink and white convolvulus or perhaps a type of morning glory. Other wild flowers stood out among the sedges and the tamarisk. Several seemed to be members of the pea family with both yellow and red flowers like snapdragons and small curled leaves to resist the extremes of temperature found in those northern deserts. Others had spiky leaves and yellow flowers, making them look like gorse or broom. There were purple, yellow and white daisies, pale anemones and a delightful small white flower with a yellow centre called snow in summer (cerastium tomentosum), which we recognized from our garden at home in Cornwall. We also saw for the first time the rare red willow of Ningxia. At this season only the stems were red but in the autumn the leaves also turn. Hares were quite common, springing up under our feet and bounding away. We also saw several dead desert hedgehogs beside the road, which must have been hit by the occasional passing lorry. We had read that they were supposed to be 'lighter in build and faster moving than their European cousins', but not fast enough it seemed.

For hour after hour we trudged on, Yin refusing to move from time to time so that Louella would have to lead him or I would drag him behind Yang. At last we reached our rendezvous, a straggle of poor homesteads on a blighted wasteland. Our minibus was nowhere to be seen and the people, not having been warned of our arrival and

Often the only people we saw during the day were migrant beekeepers, who followed the wild flowers across the open plains.

understandably fearing that we might be robbers, turned their dogs on us. We were too tired to try to explain and instead huddled behind a low wall out of the worst of the wind and driving grit while we waited.

We imagined all sorts of disasters. How would we cope if they had crashed and were all dead, or if they were simply lost and never found us? When they did turn up they were cheerful, having secured another excellent billet for us, once again in a roadmenders' compound a few miles further on beside the village of Dongwa. This time there was no hay or straw to be had, but the horses were given a pile of fresh reeds from a nearby pond and these they ate heartily.

The population here were Moslem and noticeably more relaxed and friendly. They loved Louella's Polaroid. A picture of parents holding their baby was usually all that they would accept as payment for hospitality. The disadvantage of all this goodwill was that they hated to be parted from us and burst into our quarters, a simple bare cell, furnished with two iron bedsteads. On these they sat and watched in rapt attention as we washed ourselves and our socks, cleaned our cameras and wrote up our notes. They were so amiable that we could not object to them curiously handling our possessions, trying on our watches and looking through our books and photographs. But when they spat with great deliberation and no less volume on to the floor beside our beds, it was harder not to ask them to leave and in the end we did so. Our team slept cheerfully on the ping pong table with which this well equipped compound was provided, and they were up and ready early in the morning. 'Laziness is the enemy of us all,' said Mr Li. He was having a problem conversing with the locals as they did not speak Mandarin. Only Mr Bo could understand their dialect as, although like the others he had never been in Ningxia before, he had lived for a time in Gansu, to the west.

Our hardest day now lay ahead. The road made a big detour to the south via Lingwu, crossing the Yellow River by the only bridge for many miles before turning north again for Yinchuan, the capital of the Ningxia Hui Autonomous Region. We planned to cut across country marked as empty on the map, following the Wall to a point on the Yellow River where we understood there was a ferry.

The horses seemed sluggish after their feast of rushes and gave off dreadful smells. Worse, Yang set off dead lame and I thought we would have to postpone this potentially dangerous stretch for a day until I found a stone lodged in his hoof. With this removed he was fine and Yin became the problem, lagging behind and exhausting Louella as she constantly had to urge him on. For the first hour a kindly Moslem called Han Shao Guo insisted on showing us the way across a trackless waste until we were in sight of the Wall again. Here we found a deep canyon cutting through the barren soil and, as he could ride his bicycle no further, he reluctantly left us, giving a series of anxious directions we could only sketchily follow. But how could we go wrong? There was the Wall on the skyline, its watch towers stretching to the west where the Yellow River lay some 30 miles (50 kilometres) away as the crow flies. All we had to do was follow it.

We rode down the canyon all the way to the Wall, realizing as we went that we were not following our guide's instructions, but not worried as we wanted to rejoin it. For too long we had only been able to see it in the distance and we felt, since it was the thread of our journey, that we should be closer. We were rewarded by finding ourselves in one of the most dramatic pieces of country imaginable. The whole scene was straight out of a Western set in the Nevada desert. A meandering dry river bed, with occasional pools of water where a horse might drink, lay beneath sheer sand cliffs. A steep path down through patches of sagebrush led us to the floor of the canyon where we dismounted to give the horses a rest. It was still and windless, a romantic place which we could be fairly certain no European had ever seen before. Knowing this is one of the minor self-indulgent pleasures of travel in remote places.

High above us on the far side of the river bed were clear remains of the Wall. Badly eroded forts and stretches of rampart teetered on the edge of the cliff. Much had been washed away over the centuries but enough remained to impress us once again with the incredible scale of the operation. To build a wall without any stone which would still be there five hundred years later must have demanded a vast amount of labour.

Our problems began when we tried to follow the canyon downstream to the west. The Wall was on the northern side and the cliffs there were far too steep to attempt. While it looked as though it might go fairly straight, the riverbed curved and meandered like a snake so that our distance would be doubled if we tried to follow it. Up on the plateau we should be able, we thought, to go in a straight line towards the Yellow River, and so with luck arrive that day.

Unfortunately once we had climbed up again we found that what appeared to be a level plain was networked with impassable gullies which were invisible until we were on them. Time and again we headed for a fort marking a point on the Wall far ahead, only to be stopped after a few hundred yards and forced to make a wide detour to the south. We were becoming frustrated and rather desperate that we had made no progress for an hour or so, when we came on a little cart being pulled by a mule in which sat a smiling elderly couple, the woman with a red shawl over her head. They could have been from Connemara in the west of Ireland. The man was intelligent and kind. 'Huang He,' we said, pointing towards where the Yellow River lay. 'Women yao chu Shiba Yinchuan [We want to go to Shiba (where the ferry crossed) and Yinchuan].' He shook his head and climbed down to draw a map in the sand. We must go back, he indicated, and pick up a cart track which avoided the canyons.

Now we made better time, cantering through herds of donkeys, which we thought at first were wild until we spotted the shepherds always watching over them. Once the small distant figures failed to grow into men but proved to be two very small boys of about five years old. If we had been in danger of feeling that we were pretty tough to be travelling in such a wild and inhospitable place, the sight of those two little mites resolutely rounding up their wandering flock soon put things in perspective.

From the top of the plateau we could see the extraordinary contrast this particular stretch of country presented. To our left was the great plain of central Ningxia, brushed with the green of thin grass in parts, relatively fertile, watered by occasional streams. To our right, beyond the river canyon and the Wall, which had prevented invaders reaching water, lay Mongolia, yellow with sand dunes, barren of all life. The Wall here was, in places, the provincial boundary, and it really did seem to mark the edge of civilization. Beyond lay the Autonomous Region of Inner Mongolia, where we were not allowed to venture. It looked dreadfully hard country, though where we were was desolate enough. The few houses we saw had been abandoned and there were seldom signs of modern man attempting to cultivate or tame the land. What we did see were traces of past occupation. There were dried up canals and aqueducts, ruined garrisons for the troops defending the Wall, and bare long-abandoned fields. Once we found ourselves riding along an ancient brick road which could have been Inca or Roman, but was, in fact, Ming.

There were flocks of choughs here, too, wheeling and tumbling above our heads, and nesting in holes in the Wall. Also there were several varieties of hawk hunting over the plain. The smallest had scimitar wings like a peregrine and sped low over the ground. Another sort would hover briefly before stooping on its prey.

Unexpectedly, after we had been riding for some hours, we followed a track which led to the edge of the main river canyon and there we came on a totally different scene. Below us the minimal flow of water in the river bed had been channelled and gathered to create a fertile oasis. Lush grass grew, tall poplars lined neat square fields where bright green wheat grew tall, and a low dam had been built to make a small lake. There was a mud village built into the side of the gorge and we rode down through a silent street as everyone was working in the fields. Crossing the valley at a point where the stream trickled busily over pebbles, we stopped to cool the horses' heels, but they were curiously reluctant to drink. We sensed they were near to giving up.

For a time we were able to ride along the bottom of the canyon, where there was flat, level sand and a few grassy meadows. We passed traces of a series of abandoned dams, showing that the valley must once have been fertile and well populated. It must also have been important strategically when the troops guarding the Wall would have welcomed the back-up of a farming community to supply them with fresh produce. For a time, after we had been forced out of the river bed when the going became difficult, we were able to ride along a shelf between the Wall and the cliff dropping down to the river. Once we crossed through a gap in the Wall to ride briefly into Mongolia. It was a relief to be able to do something mildly illegal without the fear of being immediately pounced on by a petty bureaucrat. Here there were no people except for occasional shepherds, and they were probably free of the Chinese compulsion to observe each trivial rule and to make sure that everyone else, especially foreigners, did so too.

From time to time the Wall and river separated and the terrain between them became impassable. Then we had to use the compass to work out the best route and as a result found ourselves leading the horses over steep goat tracks and along narrow ledges. It was spectacular country, through which we would have liked to dawdle, but the horses were so tired and the Yellow River still so far ahead. When Yang lost his shoe again and immediately became quite lame, we began to be worried if we would make it. On soft sand or grass he was quite happy, but on the hard surface of the plateau he suffered. And this was the moment when we had to leave the river and head across the plain towards our destination. We tried cutting across country, but once again ran into the problem of successive invisible gullies and so were forced to follow a stony track, which seemed to go on for ever. Both of us were now on foot most of the time, Louella dragging a reluctant Yin and exhausted by the effort. For hour after hour she had had to kick and beat him to make any progress until her ankles were painful and her arm ached. She hated herself for having to be beastly to him, was cross at constantly lagging behind and having to hurry to catch up, and obstinately determined to deal with the problem herself and not ask me to help. I was worried about Yang, who became exaggeratedly lame when we mounted to canter across open stretches of good ground and thereby try to increase our average speed. The bleak plain seemed interminable. When we came over yet another low ridge only to be faced by another stony waste with no sign of our goal, Louella burst into tears for the only time on the whole journey. We sat down, treated ourselves to a couple of slices of dried mango and some Marie biscuits and decided to swap horses, since we were both so fed up with our own mounts. Surprisingly it worked. Yang, with Louella's lesser weight, cheered up and stopped limping. Yin responded well to my fresher heels and right arm so that for a time he kept up. We began to suspect that they might have been putting on a bit of an act and were not in quite such a bad way as we had thought, although they were such miserable specimens that it was hard to tell.

We came over a final ridge and there far below us across a gently sloping stretch of desert lay the Yellow River. We fairly rollicked down to it to find our minibus and crew waiting by the little ferry. The Yellow River was wide, turgid and full of silt. The water, like that of China's other great river, the Yangze, starts in the melting snow of the high mountains of Qinghai province, bordering Tibet. Interestingly, the great rivers which start in Tibet itself, the Brahmaputra, the Mekong and the Salween, all flow into India and South East Asia. As the Yellow River passes through the loess plains it collects thirty times as much silt as the Nile, although it is 1,000 miles shorter. It has been the cause of endless flooding through the centuries, so that it has been given the name 'China's Sorrow'. Several times it has drowned a million people at a time through natural disasters or the actions, sometimes deliberate, of man. Far downstream in Henan province the silt deposited on the river bed periodically causes the river to overflow its banks and the peasants regularly build higher dykes so that today the water is in places as much as 23 feet (7 metres) above the surrounding fertile plain. When the banks burst in a flood, disaster follows over a wide area. In 1938 Chiang Kai-shek had the dykes blown up in order to halt the Japanese army's advance. A million peasants drowned and another eleven million were made homeless and starved. It was hardly surprising that the people chose the communists in preference to the Kuomintang after that.

We walked the horses on to the ferry behind a gravel lorry and our minibus, in which our team had already crossed once, and we chugged off into midstream. There we hit a sandbank and were stuck for a time as the current swirled us round and boys with poles tried to push us off. This gave us a good chance to see the dramatic contrast between the two banks of the river. Behind us, all was yellow and pale brown desert and bare hillside. The Wall came proudly through this barren land to stop abruptly at the water's edge. Only at that point were there some trees and a little cultivation. Ahead was a land of milk and honey, green from the irrigation of dozens of canals and well wooded.

The plucky little horses stood steadily through all the bumps and jolts of our crossing. Ashore, we rode them through some scrub country along the bank, which looked like the African veldt with long grass and lots of trees, to a rough road leading to the capital of the province 10 miles (16 kilometres) away. Now paddy fields stretched away on either side and it was as though the desert surrounding us since we started riding again had never been. Here, thanks to the fertile alluvial soil and the network of canals, some dug as early as the first century BC, the finest rice in China is grown.

At the first village we reached we found the very model of equestrian

The Yellow River lay between arid desert and lush, irrigated farmland. There was a small ferry, on which we were able to cross with our horses.

accommodation for our tired and sore animals. A pretty little farmhouse had an enclosure for a mule next to it. Part was roofed over, the mule was friendly and there was plenty of room for two more occupants. Quantities of good green hay were stacked nearby and the young couple who lived there seemed to know about and like horses. They helped us unsaddle and rub them down before readily agreeing to feed and care for them for two or three days. They even said they would get the local blacksmith to come and check their feet and replace Yang's shoe. It all seemed too good to be true, but better was still to come. Mr Li had booked us into the best hotel in Yinchuan, grandly overriding the predictable objections that it was full and getting us a suite usually reserved for senior officials. We were in no mood to argue as we wallowed in a hot bath and washed all our clothes. The decor left a lot to be desired; plush red overstuffed armchairs with lace antimacassars, pink nylon pillows, a hideous patterned carpet and green walls, but it was unashamed luxury and above all it was private.

MOSLEM HOSPITALITY

William Geil also reached Ningxia in June, in 1908. 'When our caravan had crossed the yellow sand and the yellow soil, it crossed the Yellow River,' he writes. 'In a triangle of land made fertile by the magic of man stands the City of Quiet Summer.' Yinchuan really means 'Silvery Plain', a name supposedly derived from the alkaline material which rose to the surface and covered the land when it was first flooded two thousand years ago. Since then successive dynasties built further huge canals, the Han (206 BC to AD 220) and Tang (AD 618 to 907) canals being the main ones used today.

In the eleventh century a mysterious kingdom called the Western Xia was set up in what is now Ningxia. It lasted for 200 years, conquered a large part of northern China and gave the Song dynasty (AD 960 to 1280) a lot of trouble. The kingdom was finally obliterated by Genghis Khan, and the name Ningxia meant that the region would be peaceful now the Xia were gone.

Very little is known about the Western Xia, but the first emperor was supposed to have had seventy-two tombs built to deceive grave robbers, as his remains were to be hidden in only one. In fact there are nine vast groups of mausoleums spread across the desolate plain to the west of Yinchuan. No one lives there now and the eroded remains of the tombs are dotted about like big brown jelly moulds on the brown plain with the brown Helan mountains in the background.

We went out to look at them, simply driving our minibus off the road towards them until gullies stopped us going further, and then we walked a mile or so up to the nearest group. Close to they were like the pyramids of Egypt, poignant in their solitude and silence. Around were masses of shards of broken green, blue and white glazed tiles, which led us to believe that they must once have been roofed or coated. Perhaps they looked like mosques, with their very un-Chinese shapes. Nobody seemed to know, though one has been excavated and we saw later in the Yinchuan museum some nice carved stone horses and bronze bulls as well as lots of complete tiles which had been saved.

Yinchuan itself is a quite attractive city with some of its walls still standing and a bell tower in the centre. There is also a smaller version of the Tian An Men, the Gate of Heavenly Peace at the entrance to the Forbidden City in Peking, and two fine tall pagodas. The 177 foot (54-metre) high fifth-century Hai pagoda has bells hanging at the four corners of each tier. These are supposed to sound like the music of heaven when a breeze blows but we were there on a still evening and heard nothing. It is a wonderfully elegant and light building and we were astonished at how well preserved it was. So many glorious treasures in China, which survived all the ravages of conquest and time, were destroyed during the Cultural Revolution, but the pagodas seem to have been spared. Perhaps they were too hard to knock down or they may have been useful for displaying Big Character banners bearing political slogans.

In Yinchuan we suddenly found ourselves being treated as heroes. The local paper carried a picture and story about our arrival on its front page two days running and a banquet was given in our honour. The day chosen was the end of Ramadan, which as Ningxia is a Moslem province was regarded as a signal honour. Most of the government of the Ningxia Hui Autonomous Region are Moslem and they would not have been able to entertain us properly during the fast, we were told.

The occasion was to be hosted by the Chairman of the province, the equivalent of governor. Fifty years before, Peter Fleming had written that 'the death rate at banquets is appalling'. Although our expectations were not that gloomy, we did not imagine that the evening ahead of us would be great fun. We were wrong, although it started slowly. As usual we were received in a large reception room with antimacassared armchairs all round the walls. Mr Hei Boli, the Chairman, and I sat at one end with his ministers next to him and Louella next to me. Like heads of state we each had our own interpreters behind us. While we made polite and formal remarks to each other, the television cameras recorded the scene and photographers took pictures.

Hei Boli looked a nice jolly man, a bit like a Chinese Anthony Quinn, but I found it difficult to sparkle as I was saving my best remarks for the speech I knew I would have to make at some point in the proceedings. Louella saved the day by leaning across me and asking him how many children he had. 'Seven,' was the answer. 'Why, you dirty old man,' she said, 'that's why everyone else in China is only allowed one now!'

There was a nervous moment as this was translated and we waited to see how he would take it. Then he roared with laughter and the general mood began to be more relaxed. Soon afterwards his interpreter was translating some lighthearted remarks of his about how lots of children would contribute to the prosperity of his small province when he was, for a moment, lost for a word. In perfect English the Chairman said, 'the word you are looking for is "development".' 'But you speak English,' cried Louella 'How wonderful!' 'Not for fifty years, I'm afraid, so I am rather rusty.' After that there was no holding us all. He took a distinct shine to Louella, gallantly escorting her into the banqueting hall on his arm and swapping jokes all through the delicious feast which had been prepared.

There were triple-coloured eggs, chicken, cabbage with cherries, duck, whole fish, lotus fruits and a host of other delicacies. We also had a chance to sample three of the five 'Treasures of Ningxia'. Facai is an edible black moss translated unromantically into English as 'black hair-like vegetable'. The subtlety of its unique flavour was lost on us but we smacked our lips appreciatively. Easier to relish were the wolfberries (*fructus lycii*), small, bright red, sweet, dried fruit, and the licorice root, both of which are supposed to be powerful aphrodisiacs, or so the Chairman told Louella. He also managed to make her eat all of the four foods which she had baulked at until then in China. She had been very brave about eating whatever we were given, accepting in general terms my theory, which has seen me safely through many strange meals in odd parts of the world, that if the locals are eating it it is unlikely to do you any harm. But she did still tend to pick over with her chopsticks the varied dishes with which we were daily presented and reject certain items. I sympathized with her about sea slugs and 'tendon', although with the eyes closed both slipped down easily and the aftertaste was pleasant. Mushrooms and yoghourt were two peculiar dislikes which she claimed to have had all her life and of which I had utterly failed to break her. The charming Chairman offered her each of the first three on his own chopsticks and her prejudices melted in a flash. At the end of the meal ice cold yoghourt was brought in stone jars. 'This is one of the great specialities of our region,' said the great man, and again she succumbed.

While this valuable flirtation was progressing, we were plied with local wine and toasted in maotai, the potent, colourless alcohol used only for this purpose. It is quite revolting and lethal, going straight to the legs. After half a dozen glasses the strongest find it hard to stand up. I had to do so towards the end of the meal, long after I had lost count, in order to make my speech. I said how honoured we were to be the first foreigners for fifty years to be allowed to arrive in Ningxia by horse. This produced a satisfactory round of applause. I got thoroughly confused describing and commenting on the three Treasures of Ningxia we had tasted but had more success when I outlined my own special interest in another, the famous soft long-stapled lambswool from the Ningxia tanyang sheep. As a sheep farmer myself at home I could appreciate the fine quality of this and said that perhaps we could do business together one day. This was not such a far-fetched idea as it must have sounded at the time, as my farming partner and I were just

In Yinchuan we feasted on local delicacies with Hei Boli, the Chairman of Ningxia Autonomous Region.

then starting the first stud in Britain of Angora goats, whose fine mohair is of even better quality.

The fifth Treasure of Ningxia is the special stone from the Helan mountains which is considered the best in China for making ink blocks, an essential part of traditional writing and painting. I had nothing useful to say about that, as although we had been round an exhibition of them that morning and were aware how highly prized and regarded they were by the Chinese, they still looked like ashtrays to us.

I presented Hei Boli with a copy of my French book and promised to come back and give him a copy of the one I intended to write about China. In return we were given a picture book about Ningxia and two fine scented medals with the white horse symbol of Chinese tourism on one side and a map of Ningxia on the other. They were impregnated with a really strong aroma of ladies' talcum powder, which the Chairman said would last for at least two years.

By the time the evening ended we were all bosom friends and barely able to stand. Anglo-Ningxian friendship had been toasted to death, Louella had shown the Chairman pictures of all our children and we had all taken Polaroid pictures of each other. We did feel very honoured as we staggered up to our room.

The next day the Director of Foreign Affairs and the Director of the General Office of the Ningxia Peoples' Government, the two senior government officials at the dinner after the Chairman, arrived in our hotel room bearing two huge bunches of red roses from Hei Boli to Louella. There was also a charming letter from him wishing us a successful completion of our journey. In it he said, 'Your visit has left a memorable impression on us,' and he praised us for 'the brilliant contribution you have made to the friendly relations between China and Britain'.

Chaos also arrived next day with the film crew, and they were to complicate our lives intolerably. In France we had strictly rationed the BBC to filming our departure, arrival and two short sequences in the middle. That film had been immensely popular and it was tempting to let it happen again in China. But our view all along had been that the ride itself came first and we would not compromise that if we could help it. This was not commercial travel from which we hoped to make a profit, nor was it an expedition to conquer the Great Wall or prove some theory. It was simply the way we had chosen to see and experience China. The justification would come, we hoped, from the money raised for the World Wildlife Fund from sponsorship.

It was quite amazing that Robbie and Debra had managed to raise the finance and get permission to make a film about us in such a short time. Once again Robbie's magic had worked and he had pulled it off in a bare three weeks.

Mickey and the Chinese film crew arrived by train after a twenty-four hour journey from Peking. Non-travellers are not allowed into the station, but we breezed past the mob of people waiting at the station gates and, looking important, managed to bluff our way on to the platform. When the big steam engine arrived pulling an endless row of carriages bursting with humanity, it stopped, predictably, against the furthest platform. The only way we could reach that, since there was no tunnel or bridge, was by climbing through the wheels under the carriages. This we and the other officials and greeters did, receiving a nasty shock when, just as several of us were underneath, the train gave a sudden lurch and moved forward a yard.

Safely on the far side we found Mickey, looking perfectly extraordinary in battle fatigues and a solar topee, unloading the baggage with the rest of the crew. Madam Xi Shang Fei, the assistant director, whom we had met with Mickey in Peking, was calm and cheerful and the young cameraman Wang Yan and sound recordist Chi Qi Xiaoyuan looked happy if exhausted by the journey. No sooner was all the baggage piled on the platform than an official came and told us that the train was not going to move and it would all have to be transported back through the carriage and across the line on the other side. This we all dutifully did and eventually, sweaty and tired as it was very hot and sunny at the station, we loaded it into a fleet of minibuses and drove back to the hotel.

We were now faced with the problem of integrating our two teams and deciding priorities. It is the very nature of filming that a great deal of time is spent having meetings and planning the next day's programme. The Chinese love meetings. At every opportunity they will gather in a stuffy room where to the accompaniment of endless cigarettes and cups of tea circular and inconclusive discussions will be held. Since leaving Peking we had managed to avoid having to attend these by the simple expedient of being on our horses all day and firmly going to bed exhausted at night. From now on it was going to be harder to escape spending our time talking about what we were going to do rather than getting on and doing it.

There was also immediate friction between our respective crews. When we suggested that Mr He might occasionally prepare a picnic lunch for everyone in the field so that they could film all day, he announced that he had not been employed to cook for so many people. We pointed out that we had only been asking him to cook one meal a day at most instead of the three for which he had been contracted and, being a good natured character at heart, he agreed. But a slight feeling of resentment persisted and we were always aware that when the film crew were around loyalties were now divided between them and us as well as between foreigners and Chinese. Everything took much longer now, too. Just leaving in the morning involved loading mounds of equipment into the film crew's vehicle or sending for members of one team or another who had disappeared – usually they were tracked down having a meal somewhere.

We all went back to the farm to find that the horses had been well looked after, the blacksmith had been to sort out Yang's feet and after four days' rest they both seemed a bit stronger. Crossing back over the Yellow River on the ferry we spent the day being filmed riding along the last mile or so of Wall. It was a superb location with pristine sand dunes stretching away into Mongolia and some good sections of mud fort near the river bank. The walkie talkies now proved their usefulness as we rode out of sight and then on cue cantered over the dunes into shot.

The Chinese attitude to film making reflected their predilection for corporate decisions and every shot was debated hotly, driving Mickey into a frenzy at times. Just when everything was ready, the clouds were right, the sun out, a passing peasant on a donkey in the correct spot, he would realize that his crew had unilaterally decided to film something else or were doing nothing. Then he would scream and shout the way all directors do at times of stress and it would all have to be set up again. Afterwards his innate charm would surface and with a rueful grin he would hug the cameraman and say, 'I'm hell to work with, I'm a bastard.' But the Chinese never apologize. To do so would involve loss of face and so the emotionally charged atmosphere always present during filming was never fully cleared away. We resolved to be patient and keep out of it as far as possible.

Our crew excelled themselves that day. After the argument about feeding everyone, Mr He prepared an outstanding feast which we found laid out in our tent in a sheltered spot out of the wind. We were none of us able to do justice to it due to the great midday heat but we praised him lavishly and then lay panting and sweating in the sun. Cold drinks would have been nice, but such luxuries are not yet part of the Chinese picnic scene. Even persuading the dining room in the hotel in Yinchuan to put a couple of bottles of orange in their kitchen refrigerator for the evening was a major battle.

Before leaving our pretty picnic site we helped dismantle and pack up the tent and then, to the supercilious amazement of both crews, we cleared up all the rubbish and put that too in bags to take home. The concept of litter being a bad thing had, we found, been omitted from the Chinese rules of correct behaviour. Even educated and otherwise quite sensitive officials we met chose to smash empty beer bottles against rocks rather than keep them; we never succeeded in training our own crew not to do this, although we did instil a sense of guilt into them, so that they tended to do it out of our sight.

In the cool of the evening we rode back along the river bank towards the ferry. This led us past the attractive walled village of Shiba. The walls must have once enclosed a large fort, and indeed this must have been a vital strategic place. Perhaps it was the very spot where Gengis Khan reached the Wall to bring about the destruction of the Xia kingdom. Now there were just a few houses inside the fortifications with generous gardens and vegetable patches. The great river ran past just outside the walls, leaving a narrow strip of land along which we could ride, looking into the village through gateways. Beyond there was a brilliant green stretch of sparse water meadow where a few donkeys and cows grazed peacefully in the sunset. It was a pastoral scene of great beauty. Half-a-dozen wild ducks flew up as we cantered past their hidden reedbed and large hares bounded off into the desert from which they had come to nibble the rare lushness.

On our last night in Yinchuan a concert of folk dancing and music was laid on for our benefit in the hotel theatre. There was an excellent eighteen-man orchestra playing an extraordinary collection of Chinese traditional instruments. As well as familiar mandolins and double basses, the string section had peculiar long-stemmed fiddles with oddly shaped sound boxes from which a noise like a Swannee whistle was produced. There were also various wind instruments, mouth organs and flutes, including some with multiple bamboo tubes, on which virtuoso solos were executed. Brilliant tiny children performed astonishing acrobatic contortions and there was a troupe of mature local dancers, the boys behaving in a camp way which would have brought the house down in Europe and could hardly have been unconscious, but seemed not to shock the audience. These Hui actors are described as having very prominent features and eyes of different colours. They certainly did not look typically Chinese. The singers were very popular, belting out what sounded like Chinese versions of Gilbert and Sullivan. The compere was a well-built girl in blue velvet with a bunch of yellow chicken feathers at her bosom, who introduced each act in a demure singsong. Mickey said he would like to buy her a drink afterwards and we were, in fact, invited up on to the stage at the end to shake the cast by the hand and share in the plaudits of the audience.

We rode south along the Huang canal. Huang means Yellow in Chinese so that the Yellow River is the Huang He. It was one of the network of canals irrigating the plain south of Yinchuan and we had been told it had a good and uninterrupted towpath, so we had a peaceful day together in refreshingly cool and pleasant surroundings. The packed earth of the towpath was an ideal riding surface and there were mature poplars all the way between us and the water.

Canals are always relaxing to ride along after the frustrations and hazards of cross country travel. There are no hills or gullies and it is impossible to get lost. There is also usually a lot of wildlife attracted by the water. That day I saw, for the only time in my life, actual flocks of hoopoes. They are usually rather shy and solitary birds, seldom seen in more than twos or threes, but here they were all over the place. With their pink and golden crests, like South American Indian headdresses, and their moth-like flight, they are the most exotic of birds and they are surrounded with legends and superstition. In the Middle Ages adding parts of them to witch's brews was said to restore eyesight and loss of memory. Like pork and shellfish they were proscribed as unclean food in the Old Testament, probably because of their filthy nesting habits – they do not clean out their nests, which become very smelly – and they even appear in ancient Egyptian tomb paintings. We had them for company all day.

There were also tree frogs, calling noisily and invisibly from the leaves above us, as well as their terrestrial cousins sounding like a dawn chorus in the paddy fields. These stretched away on either side of the canal, the groves of silvery poplars dividing the fields reflected in the still flood waters. Now we were for a while in the more familiar countryside of China, where peasants planted and weeded rice up to their knees in water, shaded by wide conical straw hats. It was a colourful scene as the women wore bright red, blue and green woollen headscarves, and vivid red shirts stood out among the usual drab clothes. There were also small patches of a brilliant blue-flowering crop which we took to be flax for linseed oil. These were often covered by a cloud of hovering white butterflies which made a pretty sight. So

Ningxia sheep being driven alongside the Huang Canal. Some of these irrigation canals were dug as early as the first century BC.

too did the yellow water lilies in the canal, though the water itself was murky and uninviting, with a good many objects floating along with the current, including the occasional dead animal.

Flocks of Ningxia sheep were driven alongside the canal to graze its banks, but we saw no boats on the water. It seemed the canals were purely for irrigation.

We lodged the horses that night at the veterinary department of the Ningxia Agricultural College at Yongning. There were two young English teachers there, VSOs whom we had been told about by the Embassy in Peking. Theirs was a lonely life. There were no other foreigners in Yongning and only two Americans and a German couple in the whole province. Although the capital had recently been opened to foreign tourists, few came and the authorities in the region were especially sensitive to the possibility of spies. Two of the Gang of Four are said to be imprisoned near Yinchuan, but the sensitivity was probably mainly because of the fear we heard expressed all along the Wall of invasion from the north by the Russians. It seems likely that the Helan mountains, which guard Ningxia's northern border and which, incidentally, mean 'horse' in Mongolian, are heavily defended. We had hoped to ride that way but had been firmly refused. A Canadian couple, who had innocently broken down near the Xia tombs at the foot of these mountains, had been the cause of a major anti-foreigner scare. As a result no Chinese were allowed to invite the teachers into their home for a meal and their movements were strictly controlled. Nonetheless they said they enjoyed teaching at the college, found the students eager to learn and planned to extend their stay.

We were glad to meet the resident vet as we were becoming very worried about our horses. Yin was now lame most of the time and needed a lot of urging to keep up, while Yang had started to develop an extremely unpleasant saddle sore on his withers. This I had treated with the purple antiseptic spray I had brought from England, which dried it up, and over it I placed a clean lint dressing each day. But it was a nasty sight and I was beginning to wonder if it was fair to make him carry on, although it did not seem to hurt him. The vet was reassuring, saying that the horses should make it to our destination near the border of Gansu; but when he looked at their teeth he confirmed our suspicion that they were much older than the rogue horse trader in Zhengjingbu had told us. Yin was, he said, well into his teens, probably sixteen, and Yang only a year or two younger. This was an added worry, not least because it would make it even harder to sell them, but we reminded ourselves that Tschiffely's horses, on which he had ridden some 10,000 miles, had been fifteen and sixteen years old at the start of his journey, and we told Yang and Yin they were lucky they had only another hundred miles or so to go.

12

CANALS AND SAND

W e now left Mickey and the film crew behind to await the arrival of Debra and Robbie with money, permits and a plan of campaign. We carried on south and west across Ningxia towards its border with Gansu, which was as far as we were to be allowed to ride on this stage. From there we would have to go by train until being permitted to mount up for the final stretch.

Much of the time now we were unable to avoid the long straight roads of China. At least they had good soft verges for the mule and donkey carts, which still greatly outnumbered the heavy lorries thundering past; but much of the time the scenery became monotonous and we needed distractions, what Peter Fleming calls 'iron rations for the intellect'. When conversation flagged and we found ourselves riding in silence we rather shamefacedly dug out our Sony Walkmans, placed them in our saddlebags and plugged ourselves in. It was extraordinary what a difference Mozart made to my spirits. Instead of slouching along thinking about my own aches and pains, while worrying about Yang's increasing reluctance to move, I happily conducted away, humming loudly to myself. Louella bopped away to her own collection of pop music. This only made the Chinese stare at us a little more intently as we passed, and some now even smiled in sympathy. If you look happy enough, even the most dour of people are forced to look happy back. We felt that we were being wafted along on a cloud of music.

There was a nice moment when, on the outskirts of a small town, we passed two telephone engineers with headphones on poring over a box of coloured wires at the foot of a telegraph pole. I grinned at them, pointed at my own earphones and asked, 'Good stuff on your set, too, is it?' Even in English my meaning was unmistakable and they laughed heartily. Moments like that bridged the cultural barrier which tends to surround all foreigners in China, and compensated for all the utterly blank stares.

We were riding parallel with the Yellow River and occasionally one or other of the canals came close to the road and we could follow a towpath again for a while. Mostly, however, the daylight hours were now spent on roads. At midday we were at least able to rendezvous with our crew, much more cheerful now they had us back to themselves, and share a better picnic than we could carry on us. It was always a huge relief to flop down on the grass and stretch out for a time, while the horses grazed and the sunshine dried their sweaty backs.

We swopped saddles as Louella's had a higher bridge which rubbed Yang's sore less. We were by now both so hardened to sitting in a saddle all day ourselves that we hardly noticed the difference, although we would both probably have objected to the idea at home.

At night we stayed in transport compounds. These were where lorry drivers and muleteers stopped overnight if they had to. The accommodation was extremely basic but there was no need to put our tent up as we were always given a couple of bare cell-like rooms and in one of these Mr He would prepare our supper. As always, the loos were the worst part, the smell hitting us as we rode through the entrance and the flies buzzing excitedly around identifying their location. Being on or near roads all day made it harder to find convenient lonely patches of scrub to visit during the day and we became scatologically preoccu-

At night we stayed in transport compounds. Basic cells surrounded a courtyard where we could tie up our horses and cook our supper.

Louella writing up her journal after a long day in the saddle. One of the things we missed most was a hot bath in the evenings.

pied. As Mickey had put it, referring to Stan Cottrell's run across China, 'We used to dream about flush toilets.'

It is a longstanding preoccupation of foreigners in China. In 1793 John Barrow, secretary to Lord Macartney, and later the virtual founder of the Royal Geographical Society, complained, 'there is not a watercloset nor a decent place of retirement in all China'.

Mr He revealed a new and most welcome talent when I complained of a stiff back one evening. Firmly laying me down on one of the hard beds he gave me a wonderfully strong and confident massage, manipulating my limbs painfully but effectively so that I slept soundly. How could we complain of discomfort when we had not only our own cook but also a personal masseur!

There was a noisy game some of the rough customers staying in these lodgings played at meals and during the evenings. It was a variation of 'scissors, paper, stone' or what we used to call at school hic haec hoc, but done with fingers extended and numbers barked out in a rising crescendo of shouts and counter shouts, which became confused and deafening. There seldom seemed to be an actual winner, just one player who outshouted the others, although we gathered that it all depended on quick mathematical reflexes so that the players never shouted numbers which, added to the previous one, made ten. The background noise of one of these games, the constant stream of the curious coming to peer through the barred window of our cell, like visitors to the zoo, and the all-pervasive smell coming from across the courtyard were the only minor inconveniences we found. Certainly there was no danger to travel in China. Surprisingly, and thankfully under the circumstances, we neither of us ever suffered from a single upset tummy in spite of all the strange and certainly unhygienic food we ate; another tribute to Mr He's skills in the kitchen.

Just south of Qingtongxia we stayed in a small place called Li Xin, close enough to the Yellow River for us to take a stroll along its banks after supper. The massive quantity of water was controlled here by a series of sluice gates, through which it churned frighteningly. Canals led off, taking foaming torrents at high speed into the countryside. Ahead upstream was a huge dam which controlled and tamed the river, preventing at least in this region the floods for which the river is notorious. It also supplied the energy for an industrial area, the chimneys and gaunt buildings of which we could see all around us. Next morning it was raining as we rode out in the early hours through this forbidding landscape. I think I have never seen a more terrible prospect, making me think of the ugliness of Britain's own industrial revolution in the nineteenth century. The smoke belching from the innumerable factories coated the ground and filled the air with noxious substances. The air we breathed was gritty and there was a strong smell of sulphur. We tied handkerchiefs over our faces, feeling like bandits in our waterproof capes and funny hats, and we rode through the glum crowds of workers trudging or cycling dutifully to their toil. Life expectancy, we thought, must be short there, and we were glad to reach the edge of the factory complex. Here we were greeted by another totally unprepossessing view: a bleak dismal countryside crisscrossed with giant pylons leading to generating stations and more factories scattering the plain. For a time we had to ride with our eyes closed, trusting the horses to follow the road, the grit was so pervasive and painful.

After a few miles of scorched earth and industrial nightmare, where nothing grew except a sort of tired broom with pink fronds, we noticed some adobe walls and the remains of ancient buildings among the pylons. Could these be outlying watch towers from the Wall in this unlikely setting? The theory was proved by the sight of a line of towers clearly marking a section of Wall along a ridge far to our right soon afterwards. It was good to feel we were back with the Wall again and from then on it kept us intermittent company. One section, which came close to the road, was made of stone; not fine-cut blocks as at the Wall's start, but definitely stone rather than mud bricks.

The main railway line also joined us for a time, when we had the pleasure of watching a succession of handsome great steam locomotives pulling endless strings of goods wagons past. Gradually the soil improved and we rode through a succession of villages surrounded by irrigated land. Here we would usually give away one or two of our handouts to people who came out of their houses to watch us. We felt that the more people who knew what we were doing the more likely we were to get help if we should need it. Sometimes a whole school would come pouring out into the road and we would be surrounded by little children running along beside us, some even daring to try out a shy 'hello' or 'bye bye'.

Once we overtook a group of young men walking along the road with sacks on their shoulders and two performing monkeys on leads. They must have been a group of strolling players who went from village to village putting on entertainments. They would certainly not have been allowed to earn their living this way during the Cultural Revolution.

We also passed a very serious bicycle race with the military in charge using official jeeps. Important men in uniform were sending off a succession of four-man teams of bicyclists in shorts and crash helmets of different colours, who pedalled furiously into the distance to reappear still going at the same speed half an hour later. Some of the teams were friendly and waved to us, but most were too preoccupied with the effort of pedalling, and for once we were largely ignored by participants and spectators alike. We almost felt slighted not to be the centre of attention.

Much more satisfactory was the occasion when a smartly dressed cadre in a rare black limousine travelling down the main road stopped ahead of us to take our picture. An ordinary peasant cyclist riding past us was so taken by the sight that he continued to look at us over his shoulder, ran straight into the official and they both tumbled into the ditch in a heap.

With irrigation and cultivated fields the bird life increased. There

Strolling players with their performing monkeys. Unlike most of those we passed on the road, they seemed not at all surprised to see foreigners on horses.

were still lots of hoopoes but these were now joined by terns, which dived into the flooded paddy fields to catch small fish, and once we saw a refreshingly English moorhen paddling about. There were swallows as well as sand martins nesting in a cliff, more crested larks, cuckoos, feral pigeons and quantities of sparrows in the roadside trees. There was also a plague of frogs one day; we found ourselves riding through shoals of baby ones hopping across the road. It would have been easy to believe that they had dropped out of the sky in the shower of rain we had just had and I almost convinced Louella that this was the case; after all, it says so in the Bible. But when they continued to hop out of the wet fields at the side she realized I was teasing.

People in Ningxia were noticeably more friendly than they had been in Hebei. Often a family riding together on one bicycle or piled into a diminutive donkey cart would ride with us for a few miles, chatting amiably about the handout we had given them. Although our conversation was still extremely limited this never mattered. Ice cream girls were plentiful and the time passed pleasantly.

On the last day Yin began to cast a shoe and at our midday stop we asked if there were a blacksmith nearby. None could be found and so I removed the loose nails and tried to hammer in two of the spare nails we had with us. I was hampered by not having a proper hammer, only a piece of iron pipe, and I am always nervous of doing more harm than

Handing out a leaflet as we passed through a village. These had been written for us in fine Chinese characters and explained that we had permission to ride along the Great Wall.

good at such moments. In the end an old man in the crowd, watching my efforts, took the pipe from me and did it firmly and efficiently. He was happy with a Polaroid picture of himself as payment.

Four days' hard riding from Yinchuan brought us to Zhongwei. Here the film crew, now including Robbie and Debra, rejoined us. There were a lot of good things to film there and we were well supported by the local authorities. Zhongwei is a strongly Moslem town and there is a thriving mosque. The elders agreed to let us ride our horses into the courtyard and pay a public and filmed visit. This suited us well, as we were unlikely to be allowed in at all without all the attendant fuss.

The imam wore dark glasses and a turban. He had a long grey beard. He and all the elders, both male and female, were extremely friendly. Although Islam seems to have fared better than other religions during the Cultural Revolution, it was still a very bad time and perhaps that was why they were so uncharacteristically welcoming to infidels. There were now, we were told, 1,800 mosques in the Ningxia Hui Autonomous Region. The Hui are the descendants of traders from the Middle East who married Chinese women and settled down in north-west China. They now form one of the five major nationalities of China with the Hans, the Tibetans, the Manchus and the Mongolians. Most of them are Moslems and about a fifth of them live in Ningxia.

The imam at Zhongwei. Most of the population in Ningxia were Moslem and they were extremely friendly.

The elders had wonderful faces; the men bearded and hawk-nosed, the women wearing white coifs over their heads like nuns, framing beautifully lined features which crinkled up into the most amiable expressions imaginable.

After tying our horses up in the courtyard we were led into the bath house, where water was ceremoniously poured over our hands from fine brass pitchers. It was one of the cleanest and freshest buildings we had seen in China and a perfect example of how the pride and reverence which were beaten out of most of the population during the Cultural Revolution are needed even in such simple things as making a bathroom pleasant. Instead of peeling walls, chipped receptacles, and a nasty smell, everything was pristine, immaculate and pure. A fine advertisement for religion and one of the most sensible aspects of Islam; the active association of cleanliness with godliness.

We were entertained in the imam's quarters, which led off the mosque courtyard. There, seated in comfort, sweetmeats were pressed on us and we were urged to eat our fill.

The mosque itself was a plain but handsome modern structure, unlike the incredible Buddhist temple we also visited. That was an astonishing, romantic building of high galleries, towers, turrets and upturned eaves, like a wooden fairytale castle. We rode up and tied our horses to two trees outside the walls. There an old monk greeted us and led us in to see the main statue of Buddha where we lit joss sticks and salaamed politely. We were able to wander through the inner courts, up flights of steps to high terraces and see the careful restoration work that was being undertaken. The paintwork on the red pillars and ceilings was being patched up where it had flaked and a man was modelling a clay figurine of a devil guardian in a side pavilion. The temple is called Gaomiao and it is unusual in that it represents three different religions. Over an archway is a sign which reads: 'At this place Confucianism, Buddhism and Taoism release souls from purgatory. Within these confines nature and man cultivate themselves.'

This admirably ecumenical sentiment disguises the fact that the religions of China have always been something of a blend. Confucianism is as much a political philosophy based on the virtue of education as a religion. As a code of behaviour it rejects the supernatural, concentrating instead on a stable social order. Buddhism was introduced from India and gradually became more and more debased as it absorbed local superstitions and traditional beliefs, especially those of Taoism, the only truly indigenous Chinese religion. At the heart of Taoism lies the desire to merge with nature. 'Wu wei' meaning 'do nothing' is its motto, the concept that action comes from inaction, like water dripping on a stone. Beginning to understand this helps the foreigner in China to cope with the frustrations of the instant 'mei you' and the bureaucratic genius for prevarication.

Our horses were lodged in a coalyard on the edge of Zhongwei. We had to sweep the ground and remove some broken bottles so that they could lie down, but we managed to obtain some straw and there was shelter so that they were not too badly off. The black beans and maize on which we had been feeding them had to be thoroughly washed to remove the dust and they were still eating well, but their condition had deteriorated badly and they were literally on their last legs. Yin, too, was beginning to develop a sore from my heavy saddle, while Yang stumbled frequently and seemed to be losing control of his hind legs.

We rode them through the centre of the town, past the inevitable bell tower and out the other side. A lane through pleasant mud-walled villages led us to the edge of a wide shallow lagoon beside the Yellow River. It was one of the most beautiful places we were to see in China, an idyllic scene of rural peace and prosperity. For once there were no intrusive overhead wires and pylons, nor any modern buildings. Instead, against a backcloth of rugged mountains across the river and a fringe of trees along its bank, a fisherman was paddling a raft made from inflated sheepskins. These craft are still used as the main form of local transport on the river, for fishing, crossing, carrying loads, cutting weed and for finding the famous facai, the edible black moss, which is gathered at night because it vanishes by day. We tried one out for ourselves. The skins are blown up like balloons through one of the

Rafts made from inflated sheepskins are still widely used for transport on the Yellow River.

legs, until the other legs and the tied off neck and rear end stick out obscenely. A dozen or so are then attached to a lightweight frame made of poles and the whole thing is dropped on the water where it floats well enough to carry two or three people for some hours. Propulsion is quite easy using a paddle dipped over the front from a kneeling position.

Next to the lagoon was a pretty farmhouse with a courtyard and outbuildings where the farmer said we could leave our horses in a fine stable. He and his family were hospitable and cheerful, letting us take over their lives while we were filmed feeding and grooming the horses, seeing to their feet, drawing water from the hand pump in the yard and settling down for the night in their family bedroom, wrapped in their colourful quilts on their kang. We ate with the family and chatted in our fractured Chinese with them. It was a pleasant interlude and wonderfully restful not to be worrying for once about our early morning start. It also gave us the chance we had been missing to experience at leisure the daily life of a Chinese peasant. Our main impression was how good it was. Certainly the work was hard and there were few luxuries, but there was an excellent feeling of contentment and family life. Two married daughters lived with the family, and there were four young grandchildren; the daughters and their constant stream of visiting friends wore pretty and colourful dresses.

Attached to a light frame the inflated sheepskins are fairly easy to manoeuvre and to carry.

Among minorities and in the countryside, the one child rule was relaxed and it was normal to see two or more children per family. Everywhere they were doted on by parents and grandparents alike.

The floors of the courtyard and most of the rooms of the low buildings round it were of packed earth, warm and mellow in the sunshine. There was also a television and, during our stay, a new washing machine arrived and was placed incongruously next to the hand pump in the yard. Young poplars grew against the walls, there were flowers in pots and a small patch of vegetables. A wooden ladder led to the roof where maize was spread out to dry. They had two cows and a donkey in one of the outhouses next to the stable where our horses lodged.

We now set about negotiating their sale. Mr Li spread the word and several potential buyers came to view. The offers we received were not encouraging and we were not in a strong bargaining position. Apart from the fact that they both now looked the aged wrecks they were, everyone knew we were due to leave shortly by train and so would have to take what we could get. After rejecting the first few sums mentioned as insulting and 'derisory' more for face than because we hoped to push the price up very far, we gladly settled for just under half what we had paid for them. They had carried us nearly 400 miles which meant that if we dropped £150 on the deal this only represented a very small cost per mile per horse, and we had no regrets.

I have to admit to few regrets as well when we finally said goodbye to Yin and Yang. The constant effort of keeping them moving had soured our relationship so that our feelings as their new owner led them off were more relief than grief. We only hoped he would get them home before they collapsed, when he might demand his money back.

All the way along the Great Wall we were made aware of the existence of desert to the north of it. The regions through which we had been riding in Shaanxi and Ningxia, and would soon be riding through in Gansu, represented the very edge of cultivable land. The battle for those living along the Wall was no longer to keep out raiding Mongols and Tartars but to hold back the sand. The single thing which had impressed us most as we rode through this barren land had been the huge efforts being made everywhere to plant trees.

After Liberation in 1949 projects were started to conserve water and plant trees in the northeast. Along what came to be known as the Green Great Wall, shelter belts were planted beside roads and between fields on the edge of the desert.

At the same time the railway system, now far the most important mode of transport in China, was being rapidly expanded from the shambles inherited by the communists. One of the new lines built then was the Baotou-Lanzhou line, beside part of which we had ridden and on which we were about to travel. This railway line, like the Wall, ran for much of its length between the desert and the green, being built often right along the edge of the dunes.

During the Cultural Revolution shelter belts were considered re-

At the Desert Reclamation Scheme in western Ningxia we saw how the sand was stabilized with straw. It produced a curious chequered look, but it worked.

visionist and most of the trees already planted were felled. Even much of the remaining natural forest was cut down, as were the poplars and red willows growing wild in the desert and holding the fragile ecosystem together. As a result the dunes began to encroach across the railway line, blocking it with driven sand. This had serious strategic as well as economic significance, as the railway would be the main means of bringing up reinforcements in the event of attack from the Bear to the north, and so something had to be done urgently. The only solution was to find some way of holding the dunes back and this the inventive Chinese had succeeded in doing.

North of us now lay the terrible Tengger Desert, off which the sand blew ceaselessly. To the west, the Yellow River made a great sweeping curve to the south and it was at this point that the railway was most constantly threatened, where it squeezed between the desert and the river. At Shapotou a major Desert Reclamation Scheme had been set up to control the situation and it had produced remarkable results.

We drove out along a rough cinder track beside the line. There was desert on both sides but close to the railway it was covered in light vegetation and had a curious chequered look to it. At Shapotou we saw how it was done. Straw is dug into the sand in metre squares and then left to rot. This both binds the sand for a time and provides some humus. The idea originally was that trees would be planted later in the squares, but the system proved to work spontaneously once the heavy labour of digging in the straw was completed. Scrub vegetation, taking advantage of the marginally improved conditions, began to sprout and a benign circle of growth slowly commenced. What we saw was the result of more than fifteen years' work in places, and the work was continuing. The first objective, keeping the railway line open, had been achieved, but just as important the infertile land on either side was beginning to bloom. In places groves of trees had been planted. Where it was possible to irrigate crops were being grown and elsewhere the land was turning green spontaneously as weeds and scrub invaded the strawbound sand. It was clearly a slow process but an effective one, and a better solution to the world-wide problem of encroaching deserts than occasional air lifts of food in times of extreme famine. Here was something for China to be truly proud of, a model and a lesson for the world. On our return through Peking I took every opportunity to say so, urging at banquets and at meetings that the information should be shared, especially in Africa. It is the beginning of a cure for what often seems an incurable problem.

The view over a steep hill of sand to the bend in the river was magnificent. We could see how the yellow sand was washed into the stream and how vulnerable the railway line running along the top must be. Down by the river I could see some tall trees and so I left the others to the view and ran down the slope to look at the little oasis where there was a small modern house beside a freshwater pond, part of the research project. As I arrived, thinking myself alone, I heard laughing voices and was surprised to see a group of young Chinese tourists arriving down another steep slope. Waiting for them at the bottom were two gaily caparisoned camels with their guardians. It all seemed rather unreal and, looking at the young people's clothes, I guessed correctly that they must be a party of students from Hong Kong; they were much too smart in their shorts and colourful T-shirts to be local. Feeling rather shy at meeting tourists, I walked over and asked if anyone spoke English. One of the girls was being helped on to a camel amid much laughter. Her friend, who was giggling uncontrollably, said, 'Yes, I do. Where are you from?' When I told her England, she said, 'Oh, so am I. I live in Hemel Hempstead.' We chatted for a time and I learned that they were on their way by train to a folk festival in Hohhot, the capital of Inner Mongolia. When I rejoined our party I enjoyed being able to say laconically to Louella, 'Sorry I took so long, but I just met a rather pretty girl from Hemel Hempstead.' No one believed me.

13

THROUGH THE
HEXI CORRIDOR

We now had to split into two parties for a while. In spite of all our efforts in Peking we had been unable to obtain permission to travel through the Hexi corridor of Gansu state other than by train. We pointed out that the railway line, the road and the Wall appeared from our maps to run side by side for most of the way, but the authorities were adamant. Only Chinese citizens could travel on the road. Our crew and the Chinese members of the film crew therefore set off in our bus for Jiuquan while Robbie, Debra, Mickey, Louella and I went by train to Lanzhou and from there through the Hexi corridor to our rendezvous. We then planned to backtrack as far as possible, acquire new horses and ride to the end of the Wall. With us came Mr Ma (which is a common Chinese name) the charming and articulate young interpreter who was attached to the film team. He had recently returned from being a student in Hawaii and we found him excellent company.

As usual it was impossible to buy soft sleeper tickets in advance for the seven-hour journey to Lanzhou but Mr Ma sorted it out with aplomb as soon as the big steam engine pulled our train into Zhongwei station at 3 o'clock in the afternoon. We were soon comfortably installed in two adjacent carriages. We puffed our way past Shapotou and round the bend in the river. From the train the reclaimed desert looked like a hessian carpet. Soon we were passing through barren hills, looking from habit for glimpses of the Wall, which should have been out there somewhere.

We saw little of Lanzhou, except for the fine range of mountains towering over the end of the main street. It reminded me of a large-scale Innsbruck. We had no time to explore as tickets had to be bought for Robbie, who had to leave us to fly back to Peking, and for our own next stage. We managed once again to secure a compartment to ourselves for the nineteen-hour journey. On the way I walked along the platform at a wayside station and looked into the hard sleeper carriage. On three tiers of narrow tightly packed bunks sprawled half-naked figures smoking and drinking beer out of bottles, which were then of course thrown out of the window. The scene reminded me of an old-fashioned opium den which I was taken to in Bangkok in 1957. With all our luggage we would have had a tight squeeze if it had been the only alternative, while the hard seats, always jammed full of passengers already, would have been physically impossible. There are times when I am glad I am no longer a student.

Once again we were pulled by a steam engine and it was a fine sight in the sunset as the train wound like a snake through high, desolate mountains. Although we would have much rather been on horses, there were certain advantages in being on a train. We could look down into some villages and see that here they seemed less spoiled than elsewhere. Several were still surrounded by a full wall and inside we could see temples and towers — once a whole series like a miniature Forbidden City. Still completely closed to foreigners, it looked good country to visit. Beside a fast-flowing stream there were clumps of wild irises in flower and a young shepherd playing on a flute. There were good-looking horses grazing the valley grass, too, and watch towers in the hills.

By dawn the Wall was there again right next to the line — packed earth, about 20 feet (6 metres) high, with traces of ramparts occasionally and some fine well-preserved enclosed forts. Sometimes it would simply vanish for a time but when there it was impossible to miss as the Hexi corridor was much narrower than we had expected. The road and railway line in the middle ran through largely bare ground with the only cultivation near the intermittent villages. To our left were the incredible Qilian Shan, catching the first sunlight on their snowcapped summits. At first sight they looked like a frontal system of white cumulus clouds, only a few miles away it seemed, soaring straight up out of the plain. They rise to over 20,000 feet (6,000 metres) and across Qinghai and Tibet to India the traveller through that hard huge region would stay on top of the world.

In spite of the spectacular view to our left, we were more interested in looking out to our right where there were some low hills through which we had glimpses of endless desert. There were patches of green in these hills and we knew from the map that the Wall would soon vanish behind them. We hoped the land it then passed through would be good riding country. First we had to rejoin our team at Jiuquan, see the local authorities and get permission to go back along the Wall and start riding again.

While waiting for them to catch us up and for the authorities to recover from the shock of our arrival, we asked the Cultural Department representative to show us some of the local sights which might be worth filming. There is not much written about Jiuquan, or Suchow as it used to be called. Marco Polo mentions Mohammedans and Christians there as well as rhubarb, for which the region is still supposed to be famous. Three intrepid middle-aged Englishwomen, Mildred Cable and Eva and Francesca French, arrived here in 1923 and spent the next fifteen years wandering in some of the least known parts of the Gobi. They were the first Christian missionaries in the region since the remnants of the Nestorians were expelled in the Middle Ages, and they seem to have been the last. They clearly loved the desert, for all its harshness, and they seem to have been motivated as much by a spirit of adventure as by the desire to proselytize. The region they went into is one of the hottest, driest places on earth and close to the farthest spot on the globe from the sea. Yet their books are full of lyrical descriptions of the landscape and they are acute observers of everything around them. Their independence, courage and lack of concern for their own comfort or safety shames modern travellers, whose horizons are reduced by the demands of family, visas and the need to earn a living. A gobi is a stone desert and they saw great beauty where others might see only barrenness:

By reason of their vivid and varied colourings these stones are one of Gobi's features of beauty, and sometimes the narrow, faint path passes through a litter of small multi-coloured pebbles, which are rose-pink, pistachio-green, tender peach, lilac, white, sealing-wax-red and black burnished by sand, sun and wind as though black-leaded, the whole, mixed with a quantity of orange-tinted cornelian, forming a matchless mosaic. One of the loveliest rock tints is a true rust, warm and glowing; and there are high jagged peaks of green shade, so soft that from a distance they seem to be overgrown with lichen, though, actually, there is not the slightest trace of vegetation on them.

They learned to find attractive nourishment in unlikely places: 'Wild chives spring up in furrows, or in fissures between rocks, and have a most delicate and pleasant flavour. The little shoots grow three inches high, fine as blades of grass, and touched with a soft bloom.'

And they observed how the inhabitants survived and tamed the desert: 'In farms which have to maintain the strongest resistance against natural encroachment, the ridge of the dune is cleverly supported by loosely knotted desert grass, and this net-like barrier is most effective in holding back the wind-lashed sand-waves.' It seems the desert reclamation scheme at Zhongwei was not as original as we had thought.

Jiuquan was the last major town on the Silk Road before the Gobi Desert and it has been a strong point and administrative centre since the Han Dynasty. It was founded by the legendary 'Swift Cavalry General' Ho Qubing, whose tomb we had visited at Xian. The Marshal Emperor Han Wudi sent him to fight the fierce northern nomads and presented him with a special bottle of wine for his personal use. After a great victory it was found that there was not enough wine for his army to celebrate with and so he poured this bottle into a clear spring from which everyone then drank. Jiuquan means 'Wine Spring'. Today the site of this legendary event, which took place not long before the general died aged twenty-four in 117 BC, has been made into a municipal park. We went there and found it to be a pretty place, with a wild feeling still. There were islands with rushes, willows where birds sang, there were dragon flies and the water was clear with lots of small fish. Once it must have been a perfect natural oasis, a rare habitat in the bleak desert, fed by underground water from the snowy mountains. Now the lake shore is lined with concrete and there are stone bridges and pavilions as well as rowing boats for hire; but for once there were no crowds and we felt that it was all done with pride.

The only other place of interest we could find a reference to in our guide books was the site of the Wenshushan Buddhist Cave Temples. We asked the Cultural Department representative if we could go there and although no one seemed to know anything about them transport was arranged. It took over an hour to drive over very bumpy roads towards the mountains, asking the way at times, until we came to a military area with a barrier across the road. The soldier guarding it was reading a comic and barely glanced up before letting us through. We found ourselves driving past rows of tanks, guns and barrack buildings. After being made to travel by train through the Hexi corridor so as not to see anything we shouldn't we were now in the middle of a major combat establishment defending China's border. We were told that it was believed by the Chinese that if the Russians were to attack from the Outer Mongolian border, beyond which their forces lay, barely 200 miles away, they could reach this point in four hours. We had a distinct feeling we should not have been there, but it was too late to turn back and we could see the caves in a cliff ahead.

The Wenshushan Cave Temples must once have been part of a great and beautiful monastery. There were traces of buildings, arches and staircases all over the hill. Inside the caves, which were surprisingly cool and pleasant, though only one or two rooms deep, there were frescoes painted on the walls and pedestals where Buddhas had stood. However, today it is a sad and rather dangerous place. The hot dry ground had been eroded so that it was hard to scramble about on the narrow goat tracks; and everywhere the Buddhist remains, which date back to the fifth century, had been vandalized disgracefully. Much of this seemed to have been done recently, the paint hacked off the faces of the figures on the walls leaving fresh chips of plaster on the ground. No Buddhas remained and everywhere there were broken beer bottles, which made scrambling about even more dangerous and indicated that the soldiers from the camp had free access to the place. There was no indication that any other tourists had ever been there. The tragedy of a country which has lost all respect for the old and the beautiful again depressed us.

The eroded and vandalized site of the fifth-century Buddhist cave temples at Wenshushan in northern Gansu. This was once a beautiful and thriving community.

From the top of the small brown mountain on the side of which the cave temples lay there was a fine view across the flat plain to the white-topped Qilian Shan. There were tank traps all over the plain and another squadron of twenty-one tanks in wraps was parked at our feet. An eagle soared overhead; the dry furrowed hillsides around us looked like elephants' skin.

Although there were soldiers everywhere, no one accosted us and we were able to walk through the village spread out along the valley next to the barracks. There were a couple of small temples with painted wooden panelling, which seemed to be in good condition. One appeared to be lived in, having glazed windows.

We drove back to find our bus arriving with both our crews exhausted after their three days' drive. They had been caught in a sandstorm and had had to hire a gang of navvies to build up the road with boulders along one stretch in order to get the bus through. Once they had recovered, negotiations began for our final stage. It was a bit like horse trading all over again, only before we could go and look for horses we had to obtain permission. We wanted to backtrack as far as possible along the Wall, which was clearly marked on the maps at this point, so as to be able to ride as far as possible along it. The authorities said at first that we were not allowed to leave Jiuquan, except to go by road to Jiayuguan. That was clearly ridiculous. There was an interesting looking river called the Hei He which flowed down from the mountains and out towards Mongolia, where it died in the Gobi Desert in some lakes. I would have liked to drive there to make a start. Later, on our way home we were to fly over this river and I was able to photograph it from the air. I saw an extraordinary line of green paddy fields between dry mountains reaching far out into the desert, but on either side was empty dune country in which it seemed horses would be unlikely to survive.

Indeed, we were now in country where there were as many camels as horses, and for a time we considered using them instead. Outside our room in Jiuquan a noisy camel pulling a cart delivered coal daily to the hotel and we knew caravans did still supply outlying oases. But we would not have been free to travel alone on camels as we were on horses, nor could we have used our good saddles.

In the end, as always, a compromise was reached and we were allowed to go as far as a village an hour's drive northeast of Jiuquan, called Gu Cheng. It was near a place called Sandong, meaning three towers, and some good bits of Wall were not far away. We decided to go there, find some horses, and spend a week riding each day. This would give us a chance to get to know the horses and for the film to be made.

We were now in country where camels were used as much as horses. This one pulled a cart with supplies for an oasis.

14

ON THE EDGE OF
THE GOBI

Gu Cheng means 'Ancient City', but the village itself was only built in 1982. It was on the very edge of the desert, on land which could be irrigated via a tree-lined canal, but which was dry when we arrived. Between the village and the first dunes lay an open area of meadowland through which a stream ran. After rain the grassland flooded and shallow lakes formed; without rain the stream dried up.

On the meadow flocks of sheep and goats, some cattle, horses and camels grazed. There were good stretches of mud Wall beside and through the dunes, and stark watch towers were silhouetted on a high ridge. It was a perfect location. Beyond the dunes there was another grassy plain, less fertile here, the vegetation struggling against the sand. Beyond that there were more sand hills and then nothing but empty stony plains and dunes as far as the eye could see.

Looking back towards the village all was green and lush. Poplars had been planted everywhere around the houses and fields so that the countryside seemed wooded. Above rose the southern mountain barrier, which made the community's existence possible. The water from the huge perpetual snow fields was not far below the ground. Every house had in its yard a hand pump from which beautiful ice cold water was drawn.

We based ourselves on a family called Han, who were extraordinarily tolerant of the way we and the film crew messed them about. Mr He took over their kitchen to cook meals for us all, which we ate in their courtyard. We stored our saddles and other equipment in one of their rooms, we washed at their pump; the only thing we did not do was sleep there, although we were invited to do so. It was easier all round to commute daily from Jiuquan and we really were too many to impose on them full time. Instead we descended on them each morning and disrupted their lives, often until far into the night.

The layout of the Han house was much the same as that of the one we had used beside the Yellow River. Although here in the far north-west the lifestyle was simpler, there being no electricity, television or washing machines, it seemed in some ways even more comfortable and well organized. The yard was swept immaculately each day and a good crop of vegetables grew in the centre. Chickens and pigs – these people were not Moslems – were kept in their place, either in pens or in the back yard. I wandered through into this on our first day and was greeted by a scene straight out of a Bethlehem nativity play. In a thatched stable against the mud wall were a donkey, a cow and two goats eating from a manger. A sheep with two young lambs lay at their feet next to an old fashioned wooden waggon with long shafts. A pitchfork with wooden prongs was stuck in a pile of straw where chickens scratched. Beyond was an arched gateway through which there was a view of poplar trees in rows leading to the plain; Leonardo da Vinci's dream background.

Feeling safe in such familiar surroundings, the subject of innumerable Christmas cards, I strolled on. Suddenly a small boy who had followed me began to shout and gesticulate urgently. I turned and there was such terror on his face as he pointed at something behind me that I leapt towards him without even looking over my shoulder, imagining a snake or giant monster about to pounce on me. At that moment a large black dog jumped out from behind the archway and flung itself at me, snarling and snapping, to be brought up short by its chain inches from my retreating backside. Everyone laughed when my young saviour and I returned to the front courtyard and told them about it, but it could have been nasty and I was grateful to him.

The people here being considered a 'minority', the one child rule did not apply to this area. Three children were allowed and there were practical advantages in having this number. Throughout the region the farmland was allocated according to the number of family members. Here, where there was plenty, they received three mu each (15 mu equals 1 acre). In Jiuquan, where land was in short supply relative to the population, they only got 1 mu each. An average family of five in Gu Cheng would therefore have an acre to work. This was a lot considering Chinese farming methods, which are more like what we would call gardening. This did not, of course, include the free grazing on the open plain. Children born beyond the permitted three were considered 'non people' and were given no papers. We were told that everyone hoped that the rules would be changed by the time they were grown up.

Ever since arriving in Ningxia we had been seeing an increasing number of people with relatively non-Chinese features, such as curly hair and hooked noses, though most were clearly the product of inter-breeding with Turks and Uighurs rather than pure blooded. The minorities who traditionally inhabited the northwest have had a very tough time over recent centuries and many were wiped out or absorbed. Meanwhile colonists from other distant parts of China were moved there. Some were brought in to help build the Ming Wall in the sixteenth century, others were sent from disaster prone areas, such as flood victims from Henan. Mr Li said, 'They have come to settle these inhospitable regions. They are like your Australians.'

Gu Cheng seemed to be a happy and contented village. The main street, which was lined with young poplars to shade the courtyards along it, was swept daily. The villagers could buy their houses for 2,000 yuan (about £400), perhaps two years' total income. They told us that although it was quite cold in winter there was sun most days in which the old people could sit for a while out of the wind in their courtyards. They knew whether it was going to be cold enough to warrant lighting the fires under the kangs by watching the snowline on the mountains. When it dropped below a certain point that meant it was time to start the central heating.

Our first task was, as usual, to find ourselves some horses. We walked to the far end of the village and stopped outside a house where a man was having his head shaved. His pate was quite blue when exposed and he grinned sheepishly up at us. Down an alley next to the house we saw a nice-looking grey tied up. Louella, having drawn the short straw with Yin last time, took a liking to it and claimed it for her own. It appeared to have an amiable character, though I thought it rather long in the tooth and put its age at fourteen or so. The young wife who owned it assured us it was eight. We seemed to have heard that before, but accepted it nonetheless in principle. On his left flank the Chinese character for 'middle' was branded. This is the same character as that used for 'China', deriving from the Middle Kingdom.

A quite frisky bay with dark eyes was then led out and tied to a tree. I walked up to him and gently laid my hand on his neck. He threw his head up, snapped the rope and escaped. So much for impressing the locals with my way with horses. Fortunately he did not try to run away but allowed himself to be caught at once. I put a halter on and led him up and down the street. This he accepted, though the sight of me clearly alarmed him. I was not sure if he was just shy of strangers or if my being a European had anything to do with it. I asked his owner to bring some food and a bowl of black beans and maize was produced. He accepted this from the bowl but would not take it from my hand. I had a distinct impression he had been hit around the head as he was very nervous of fast movements, but he was definitely much younger than the grey and I accepted his owner's claim that he was seven years old as not being a huge underestimate. He had good sturdy forelegs, though rather less impressive hindquarters, and both horses were in far better condition than any of our previous mounts. We decided they should be able to stand the two weeks' hard riding we had in store for them.

The next move was to try them out. While we tacked up, Mickey,

We called our last two horses Marco and Polo. On them we were again free to explore the edge of the Gobi desert.

with an alarming burst of enthusiasm, told his crew to get ready to film. 'This could be good,' he said. 'Robin might get thrown off. Stand by!' To his evident disappointment both horses behaved sedately and I even had trouble persuading mine to break into a canter until I cut myself a switch of poplar. Louella was delighted to be riding something again which did not feel as though it were about to collapse beneath her. We blew into their nostrils and we called them Marco and Polo. Marco was just 14 hands and Polo 13.2. We agreed to hire them at 10 yuan a day, as it would only take a couple of days to ride them back along the road once we had reached our destination.

We set off for our first proper ride on our new mounts. Both of them were hard to manoeuvre. Marco needed the stick I had provided myself with in order to get him into a canter, but then he loped along quite well, although he was not as fit as I had expected and worked up quite a sweat. Polo made a lot of fuss about stopping, throwing his head about and nearly falling over if pulled up sharply. They both had very bad mouths, but since most of the time we were giving them their heads that did not matter much. The village street ended at the edge of the open grassland with the dunes and horizon beyond. We cantered across past grazing animals, stopped at a stream to let the horses drink, and rode up into the dunes. We felt free at last of the atmosphere of

Mr He, our cook, was a natural performer. Always cheerful he was an expert in martial arts and so ready to protect us as well as producing delicious meals from very basic ingredients.

travelling in a group and the problems of needing permission to do everything. Our spirits lifted and we were tempted just to keep going across the Gobi to whatever lay beyond. Instead we let our horses race each other home, only slowing up to walk the last mile or so into the village. There, as soon as they were unsaddled, they both rolled in the dust, which we felt was a good sign that they were feeling well.

From now on we were free to explore a different bit of the countryside around Gu Cheng each day; to follow half-hidden stretches of Wall and ride to distant watch towers in between bouts of filming. These became more demanding as the film team tried to pack into a couple of weeks the whole story of two months' riding.

Mr He proved to be a natural performer, quite unselfconscious in front of the camera and full of unexpected talents. While being filmed preparing food for us all at a camp in the desert he sang jolly Chinese folksongs, slicing onions in time to the music and throwing spices into the pot with panache. We lay on the sand alongside, cleaning our tack and listening, while above us a row of friendly local maidens in coloured wool headscarves watched and giggled.

Mickey directing was a stranger sight than those on camera. He was wearing baggy camouflage trousers with elastic ankles to protect his legs from the sun, his white arms in a skimpy T-shirt contrasting with his pink face under the straw solar topee. Around his neck were slung several cameras, a fur-covered water canteen and a bright yellow beach radio. Another water bottle and several pouches were attached to his belt and with all his appendages he tended to clank and stumble as he moved. But for all his shambolic appearance he was a dynamo of energy, constantly chivvying the camera crew to set up new scenes and trying to catch the spirit of what we were doing. We enjoyed his company hugely and hoped that in spite of all his difficulties his talent would show through in the final film.

Debra, in the role of producer, looked more the star than any of the performers. Always fashionably dressed in colourful casuals, her hair tied up and with dark glasses perched above her forehead, she would have seemed more at home in St Tropez. Her skin was always oiled, her legs were tanned beneath her short shorts and she carried a sophisticated array of pills and potions with her, but she was tougher than she looked and never complained about the fairly primitive conditions in which we were living.

The surroundings of the village were picturesque in different ways. The shaded lanes, where rows of trees gave a distinctly French feel to the landscape, were perfect for riding along in dappled sunlight. Decorative peasants in straw hats and headscarves, looking more like fashion models than the labouring proletariat, led little donkeys pulling carts. Others headed for the fields with hoes over their shoulders chatting merrily as though on their way to the shops. There was little sense of toil. Even the bearded old men smiled at us and the little rosy-buttocked babies positively squealed with glee when Louella cuddled them.

We went to visit the school, riding up just as the teacher, who happened to speak good English, was marshalling his class at the entrance. We all greeted each other and the teacher prevailed on us to dismount and visit his class. There were thirty children aged between eight and ten, the boys in their caps and most of the children of both sexes wearing red Young Pioneer kerchiefs. Millions of primary school pupils belong to this organization, which is similar to the Boy Scouts in that it undertakes community projects. Selection is supposed to be by ability and during the Cultural Revolution they were known as 'Little Red Guards'.

Seated at uncomfortable little desks below walls bare of decoration, they were perfectly behaved and chanted dutifully line by line the story which was read out about Giant Pandas, international friendship and conservation. It seemed oddly appropriate in view of our fundraising efforts for the World Wildlife Fund, but we could see from the well-thumbed books they were using that it was today's lesson. Predictably, the film ran out halfway through this charming scene and we were all faced with a wait of an hour or so while more was fetched. The time when the children normally broke for lunch had passed and anxious parents were gathering outside to fetch the smaller ones. It looked as though we would lose them, but at that moment Mr He stepped into the breach. First he sang them a song and then he made the children join in. He was so funny and so good at making everyone relax and laugh as he conducted and clowned about that they loved it and the time passed in a flash. It was just a pity there was no film to record this.

It was Louella's birthday on 25 June. We spent most of the day charging about the countryside on our horses in front of the cameras. The whole place was like a film set, with adorable foals next to their tethered mothers. We found a nice man living in a small hut guarding a fish pond. He told us people would come and steal the fish if he were not there. We could see the fish moving in the water when he threw a bundle of weeds in to feed them. They seemed to be about six to eight inches long.

In the Han courtyard Mr He was preparing a surprise feast for Louella. There was a huge communal chicken stew and endless side dishes. Everyone in the village came and went to see how the foreigners behaved and to sample the Peking cook's creation. They were impressed by the quantities of beer consumed by the film makers as this was a luxury which seldom reached the village. I was at the time reading a book about the great eighth-century poet Li Bo, one of the undisputed geniuses of Chinese literature, who was a famous drinker. I gained much face by getting Mr Ma to translate for the assembled villagers a passage where the Tang dynasty was referred to as 'an age when, among specially talented people, drunkenness was universally recognized as a state of perfect, untrammelled receptivity to divine inspiration'.

In Jiuquan I had managed to get a revolting pink sticky cake and to find thirty-five tiny candles to go on it. This caused a lot of interest and there was a resounding cheer when Louella blew them all out in one go. They all tried a bit of cake and congratulated her. Everyone in the village was smiling and ready to make friends. The teenage boys were particularly forward, even a little cheeky at times. There was one boy who had become a special friend. He had a sensitive squashed face and regularly called me by my name, Lo Bin. Mr Ma told us that his name was Liu Bin Xian, which sounded much like my name at the start, and that he was a talented young painter. We went to visit his home and he produced his collection of works. They did show talent but were, as he said himself, quite unskilled as he had had no training. He insisted I choose one for myself and he gave Louella a picture of Jiuquan Park which he had done especially for her birthday. There was a message in his good calligraphy along the side which read: 'Wishing Mrs Han Lo

Bin a Happy Birthday.' He had also copied out, since the birthday party, a poem by Li Bo.

> If Heaven does not love wine
> The vinous stars would not be in the Heaven.
> If the World did not love wine
> The World would be without Wine Spring City.

I promised Liu Bin Xian that I would keep in touch with him and that I would try to see if he could get a scholarship of some sort. It seemed such a pity that a boy like that, clearly desperate to develop his talents, should be unable to do so. I knew he saw his meeting with us as a chance to join the world he longed for outside, where people would recognize the value of painting rather than laugh at him. There was not much we could do, but we told the British Council in Peking. They do have scholarships to help Chinese students and even if he did not qualify, the very fact of his being enquired about might draw him to the attention of the local authorities and make something happen. Mr Ma said he would try and help as well by mentioning him in Jiuquan.

That night there was a storm with heavy rain and the plain was flooded with shallow lagoons. We wondered how the fish guardian stopped his charges simply swimming away. The horses enjoyed splashing through the water, which was warm from the hot sand. In the mountains snow had fallen and lay halfway down the slopes, quite beautiful in the fresh morning sunshine.

In one of the ponds, concealed from the village by a dune, we came across eight of the children from the school frolicking naked in the shallow water. The four girls were extremely pretty water nymphets to a western eye, but the scene was of perfect innocence and they were happy to be photographed. They splashed each other and our horses, then lay in the sun to dry. They were neither amazed and overcome by our unexpected arrival, nor embarrassed by being watched at play. In a country where the normal overcrowding as well as political and social controls tend to make everyone selfconscious and conformist, it was wonderfully reassuring to stumble on children behaving as they do anywhere in the world. It remains one of our happiest images of China.

One day we were caught in a dust storm far out in the desert. The wind blew huge quantities of sand horizontally across the ridge along which we were riding. It stung our faces like needles. The force of the storm increased until we were barely able to move, even walking and leading our reluctant horses. There was no danger of our being lost as we knew we had only to follow the compass to the south to reach farmland again but it was frightening and uncomfortable, the sand hurting relentlessly and penetrating our clothes, mouths, eyes and noses. Staying close together we battled on for a couple of hours. At times the wind was so strong that we had to lie down, while the horses turned their backs to the storm and we held them by their head ropes.

With the combined effort of wind and sand, rain and man's deprivations, it is extraordinary that any of the Wall has survived in these regions, and yet we found some quite well preserved sections. At one of these there was even a large cut stone with Chinese characters carved on it. They read, 'Watch Tower of the Great Wall. Important Cultural Relic. Anyone damaging or removing them will be liable to prosecution.'

On our last night in Gu Cheng we all went up into the dunes to film a camp fire scene. We had brought a bucket of dried camel dung with us to make a fire. Over it we suspended our kettle on a couple of forked sticks. We made ourselves some coffee, lay back against our saddles wrapped in our sleeping bags and talked about the two months of riding which lay behind us. Louella mused on all the nice, kind people we had met and how lucky we were to have seen so much of the Wall, something most people only read about. The restored sections in the east were magnificent and everyone who saw them was impressed. But now as we approached the western end we had a sense of the incredible scale of the building operation it represented. It is often said that it is the only man-made object visible from space. In fact this is said so glibly that I strongly suspected it to be a myth. I wrote to NASA to ask if any astronaut had ever reported seeing the Great Wall of China from space. In his reply the Chief, Special Events Branch, said:

This is in response to your letter asking for information about what can and cannot be seen from outer space.

First, we must define space. From low earth orbit, (200–300 miles) which is the range of the space shuttle above the earth, astronauts have seen and photographed waterways, highway systems and many of the large cities of the world, i.e. Tokyo, New York, Los Angeles.

However, recurrent reports that astronauts have seen the Great Wall of China from space cannot be substantiated. In fact, it would be difficult, if not impossible, to see the Great Wall from space because over the centuries the Wall has become overgrown with vegetation which causes it to blend in with surrounding terrain.

Astronauts who flew during the Apollo missions to the moon reported that as their spacecraft broke the bonds of earth and began its lunar journey, the earth got smaller and smaller and soon they were only able to distinguish the white of the clouds, the blue of the oceans and sometimes, depending on the degree of cloud cover, the brown and green of the continents.

In fact I believe this myth goes back to the calculations made by Captain Parish in 1793, when the mathematics of the time indicated that the Wall's sheer length *should* make it visible from the moon. Another myth probably contributed to the idea being universally accepted. There is an ancient Chinese legend that the Emperor Qin rode up to the moon on a magic carpet. From there his newly unified nation looked vulnerable and so he decided to build the Great Wall.

As we lay in the still desert night drinking our coffee out of tin mugs beside a camel dung fire, we could see a short section of the Wall outlined against the sky. A Bactrian camel with a rider safely slumped between its two humps padded past, turning its head to look down superciliously and snort at the strange sight of us. The night was still and we heard a desert fox as the full moon rose unexpectedly behind the Wall. We were content to be there.

15

THE END OF THE WALL

The day we reached the end of the Wall was among the hardest and most exhausting of all. Leaving the film crew to have a lie in, we had groomed the horses and saddled up by 7 a.m. We were determined to try and follow the Wall as far as possible and this meant heading out into the desert to the north. Through Mr Li we received conflicting advice which delayed us and was frustrating as we were anxious to be off while it was still cool. He had trouble understanding the local dialect and, like all our relatively cosmopolitan team from Peking, found the peasantry inferior intellectually. 'I am dull from dealing with these sort of persons,' he said. When we tried to pin down specific information on directions he would say, 'Nobody can tell,' which made us grind our teeth as our lives might well depend on not getting lost.

We left through familiar country, across the plain and out to the dunes. It was a lovely morning, with a red dawn sky, fresh with a light breeze and even some dew glistening on the coarse grass. We followed a piece of Wall we knew already, then left it to head by compass further out than we had been before and so, we hoped, cut a wide corner. There were several dry riverbeds to cross, the final fingers of flash floods from the mountains, which sometimes poured down into the desert to vanish under the sand. One of these looked suspiciously damp and luckily I slowed Marco up as we cantered across it. In a moment he was sucked into a quicksand. I stayed in the saddle as he floundered back to the bank and was just able to leap ashore holding onto his reins. Then I pulled and shouted, urging him as he struggled. For a moment I thought of plunging in to release his saddle so that at least that would be saved if he disappeared – Camargue saddles, being designed for horses which are constantly in and out of marshes, can be freed by a quick pull on three thongs – but then his feet came in contact with firm grass and he managed to drag himself out. His flanks were heaving but he was unhurt.

We found a safe way across by following some camel tracks and continued on our westerly bearing. This took us back to human

With an absence of landmarks towards the western end of the Wall, it was necessary to take compass readings.

habitation, a series of pleasant villages isolated on the edge of the desert and irrigated by canals. Through these ran a cart track, dead straight for several miles and in exactly the direction we wished to go. To our right we could see signs of the Wall from time to time out in the dunes, and far ahead we began to make out the Black Mountains which guard one side of the Jiayu Pass. Things were looking pretty good at 11 o'clock when we stopped to give the horses a brief rest under some trees where the cart track ended. Ahead lay an open stony waste with a curl of smoke beyond it which indicated Jiayuguan, our destination. A friendly local assured us we could ride straight there and we set off optimistically. Four hours later we felt as if we had made no progress at all. The plain was far more uneven than it appeared, and a great deal bigger. Out in the middle all the horizons vanished and we were surrounded by mirages. For some time a surrealist factory had been visible dead ahead, smoke belching from its tall chimney. This was now reflected upside down in what appeared to be lakes of water and for hour after hour it seemed to get no bigger or closer. I felt an unfamiliar touch of agoraphobia, panic that we would never reach sanctuary again.

The horses found the going on the hot sharp stones painful and they were tired and disillusioned, so that for much of the time we walked. Both our pairs of boots were by now wearing out and in need of repair.

Polo was quite stout-hearted and plodded gamely on, but Marco felt as if he were about to give up. Now it was my turn to lag behind and to have to urge my mount every yard of the way.

Then, totally unexpectedly and without warning in that dry wilderness, we came on a deep concrete canal sunk into the ground, along which raced a torrent of muddy water. At first it was a refreshing sight until we realized the water was out of reach for the horses to drink and that we would have to make a wide detour in order to cross. At last we found a bridge and were able to continue. A second canal an hour later gave us more trouble. We could find no bridge, only a sluice gate where a couple of narrow steps led around the corner high above the water. Marco walked up them sensibly, but when Louella came to lead Polo over them he took a huge leap and landed squarely on top of her. For a time it looked as though he had broken her foot, which was very painful. But after a while she was able to wiggle her toes again and so she bravely said she was all right, mounted, and carried on.

Another couple of hours of hard slog and at last the factory began to loom large ahead, two black slag heaps bracketing it so that we did not have the energy to try to ride around. It was hardly the ending we had expected for our romantic ride along the Great Wall, but at least there would be water there for the horses and we would be able to get directions for the fort. Some of the chimneys were pouring out black smoke, others pungent yellow and a rather sinister off-white, which smelt deadly. After total solitude for six hours we were plunged into a bizarre world where gigantic gantries towered overhead, grotesque pipes bulged and leaked carrying hot liquids between huge tanks and boilers, sudden bursts of steam were released, and deafening bangs, shrieks and whistles rent the air. Fortunately the horses were too exhausted to react but we found it hard to stay calm and confident.

Some friendly labourers gave us directions, pointing out a route through the heart of the industrial complex, which we deduced was an iron and steel works. We crossed a network of railway lines, dodging between a couple of noisy steam shunting engines, and came to an even worse man-made desert of slag and rubbish. Beyond this we found gates through which we rode, to be stopped firmly but politely by an official. In spite of our urgent protestations that we were in a hurry and just wanted to reach the fort, he insisted that we dismount while he telephone for instructions. There had been talk of an official welcome with the governor of Jiayuguan and the local press turning out to greet us and we did not want to keep them waiting, but explaining this was beyond our ability in Chinese. Instead he put a kettle on and told us to sit down and wait while it boiled. He read our handout through, then read it aloud slowly over the telephone. We found a tap and watered the horses, as a dreadful sense of anticlimax began to overcome us. Then we looked at each other and began to laugh. Here we were, buoyed up by the prospect of reaching the end of the Wall, expecting the plaudits of the local population and perhaps the world's press as we rode in triumph through the final gateway, only to find ourselves stuck in a dingy office, held prisoner by a kind man who was only doing his job. We dared not argue too vehemently as we strongly suspected that such an important factory would be closed to foreigners and that we should not be there.

He gave us glasses of boiling water which took an age to drink and at last he let us go, even sending a lad on a bicycle to guide us through the maze of roads between the factory buildings. We had never received the official permit we had been promised for the walkie-talkies and I was a bit nervous of using them in such an obvious security area. However, having failed to make contact with the others all day, I thought I should try again and so pulled the transmitter out of my saddle bag and slung it round my neck. Just as I raised it to my lips there was a roar of engines and a convoy of twenty police motorcycles overtook us. Each one had an armed man on the pillion and a sidecar in which sat another holding an automatic rifle pointing up at 45 degrees. This meant that I looked down the barrel of each one as they passed. Tired after a day in the saddle and dazed by the din and smoke around us, it seemed like a judgement and I felt sure we were going to be arrested. At that moment the handset gave a squawk and I could hear Debra's voice calling us. 'Hold on,' I whispered urgently into it, 'We're surrounded by the police and can't talk.'

Soon after we passed out through the main gate without being challenged by the battery of armed guards there, who just stared at us in amazement. Riding out of that inferno of blast furnaces and smoke stacks we must have been a most unexpected sight.

We were now, we discovered, in one of the main streets of the new city of Jiayuguan and so we agreed on the radio to meet the others at the central roundabout. There a gratifyingly large crowd gathered round us and we were able to start a small riot by giving handfuls of our handouts away. We were not going to need them again. The people went mad for these, snatching them from our hands and fighting for them like dogs over a bone. It was an extraordinary example of mass hysteria, which we were able to watch in safety from our horses. As we rode off in the direction of the fort we saw the police arriving in some force. We thought they were coming to quell the unruly mob, but we later learned that they simply arrested the film crew and their driver for parking illegally while they filmed the scene. There was virtually no traffic in the town, but there were strict rules about where it was allowed to park and they had transgressed. It took them an hour to sort it all out down at the station.

It took us an hour to ride out of town and up to 'The Strongest Fortress Under Heaven', now clearly visible ahead, rising out of the plain between the mountains. It has always been a place of great strategic importance to China, lying in a narrow pass between the Qilian Mountains to the south and the Black Mountains to the north. It was the western end of the Ming Wall and it guarded the entrance to the Silk Road into China proper. Through this fortress almost every foreigner entering China overland had to pass. Beyond it were the bad-lands to which Chinese citizens were exiled if they offended their Emperor. Travel documents were needed to pass through and a garrison of 1,000 men was retained there to see that the law was upheld.

We had started at sea level at Shanhaiguan. Jiayuguan is at 5,817 feet (1,773 metres). The fort looked more magnificent than the First Pass Under Heaven at Shanhaiguan and we found it to be largely restored. At each of the four corners of the fort there is a turret and the 30 foot (9 metre) high walls are crowned by regular crenellations. The two great gates at the eastern and western entrances are 56 feet (17 metres) high and beautifully decorated, with painted pillars and carved beams below their curled eaves. Below these run brick-lined archways, like dark tunnels 66 feet (20 metres) long guarded by great wooden doors wrapped in iron sheets and painted black. The parapets, gates and towers were built of mud bricks, but the walls were simply rammed earth made by a special process which gave them the immense strength needed to survive until the present day. The yellow

'The Strongest Fortress Under Heaven': Jiayuguan.

earth was carefully sifted, dried and cleaned of all weeds and seeds. Then hemp, lime and glutinous rice were mixed with it to create a strong cement. Each stretch of wall was tested by having an arrow fired at it: if it bounced off, the wall was passed; if it stuck in then the job had to be done again. The fort and its surrounding defences were built by the Ming Emperors between 1485 and 1593.

In the last few hundred yards of the Wall we had been following on and off for nearly 2,000 miles (3219 kilometres), right under the shadow of the fort itself, lay a small farm. One side of its courtyard was the Wall and against this there was a stable. Here good old Mr Li had arranged that we could leave the horses; the perfect place. We fed and watered them there and quietly congratulated each other on having made it.

Although we had reached our destination we still had a couple more days of filming. The next morning we rode out along the continuation of the Wall beyond the fort. This is known as the 'Open Wall' as it runs in full view across a flat gravelled plain towards the Qilian Mountains. The 'Hidden' Wall runs to the Black Mountains along a slope beneath a hill north of the fort and it cannot be seen either from the fort itself or from the plain below. It was along this stretch of Wall that we had hoped to arrive, but we had failed to find it and had instead been directed to the centre of the nearby town.

Now we rode south along the 'Open' Wall. We found it to be very well preserved, as much as 13 feet (4 metres) high in places and running straight as a die for 5 miles (8 kilometres). At the very end there was a watch tower and as we rode up to it we came to what was without a doubt the most spectacular place we had seen since leaving the sea. A gigantic canyon lay between the desert and the mountains, its sides dropping 300 feet (91 metres) sheer to the Taolai River below. It was the most impregnable end to the Wall imaginable and completely unexpected. We had known the Wall must end somewhere there as its final role was to bar the valley, but we had vaguely assumed that it would meander off up into the mountains much as it did at Shanhaiguan where it began. Instead here was vivid proof of how effective it must have been at keeping everyone out of China. Although its walls were crumbling, the last watch tower, perched on the very edge of the canyon, illustrated more clearly than all the books that we had read about it that the Great Wall meant business and there was no way round.

The only thing spoiling the moment for me was that I was overcome by an acute attack of vertigo and could barely move. I became convinced that Marco was going to step off the edge and Louella, who is fortunately fearless about heights, had to lead me along the edge and stay between me and it as we were filmed. Directly across the valley from us the mountains rose steeply up from the river bed. In one gulley

'We made camp under the wall with some singing camel drovers.'

opposite a shepherd stood guard over his flock of sheep, but otherwise it looked harsh, impenetrable country. A cormorant, white feathers showing below its steadily beating black wings, flew past us at eye level. I averted my eyes from the space below us and felt sick.

That night, for the cameras, we made camp under the Wall with some singing camel drovers. A large straw bonfire was built, three bad-tempered camels, two males and a female, were persuaded to group themselves around us, and the three singers sat together on a straw bale as Louella and I reclined against our saddles and watched. The lead singer had a wall eye and wore a white skull cap. He was a Moslem, a Hui from Ningxia working on the restoration of the fort as a bricklayer. He was a good singer, using Chinese words to Turkish music, the strange wailing rhythm perfect for a desert night. 'The most beautiful flower is the white peony; the most beautiful man is a young boy,' he sang, his white eye glinting evilly in the firelight. The magic of the setting captured us and we gave ourselves over to the moment, enjoying the sensation of desert space, peace and beauty to the full. Would that more of the time could have been like this, that we could have been allowed to sleep out in the desert under the stars. We felt the irony of being prevented from doing so in one of the safest countries on earth, where crime is punished ruthlessly and opportunities to enjoy ill gotten gains do not exist.

It was almost over now. We had done what we had set out to do, but we felt no 'braggart mood', knowing how little we had really achieved or suffered, compared with the great transcontinental journeys of history. But then I recognized the familiar hollow sense which always awaits the traveller at his destination, the aftermath of Stevenson's hopeful travel.

One more tiring ride lay ahead of us. We had to return the horses to Jiuquan and this meant hours of painful roadwork on our exhausted animals, until we reached a stable from which their owners could fetch them. Just before the end Marco gave up and refused to go on. Dismounting did no good and in the end we were dragged into town by Louella, Marco's head rope tied to her saddle. She said she felt like an Amazon bringing home a captive. I just felt foolish and the Chinese laughed to see my loss of face.

We went to the market, strolling through the astonishingly varied stalls. Ducklings and chicks were crowded in high-sided trays like clockwork toys; goats, sheep and cows were tethered along a wall. Raw meat attracted swarms of flies, all sorts of exotic spices added their peculiar perfumes to the air. There were vegetables in profusion, sacks of animal feed, seeds and nuts, clothing stalls, trinkets and plastic sandals; it was a thriving busy place.

As we were leaving Mickey said, 'Hey look, there's a racoon!' I looked and saw a young badger tied by its hind leg with wire to a bicycle. There was a crowd round it and it was trying desperately to escape, scrabbling to dig a hole in the hard dusty ground. I tried to walk on and not interfere, but it was impossible. Badgers are rather special to me as there are a lot on our farm in Cornwall and I have fought with the Ministry of Agriculture to prevent them being exterminated under the mistaken eradication programme. The World Wildlife Fund had supported me in the battle and I had even written the foreword to a new book about badgers, written by Richard Meyer, who had made a three-year study of the supposed badger problem for them. We had undertaken our ride partly to raise funds for the World Wildlife Fund. How could I ignore a captive badger?

I quickly explained the situation to Mr Ma and asked him to help me. He at once responded with more enthusiasm and understanding than I could have dared hoped for. 'Why are you selling that animal?' he asked its owner.

'It will make good eating and its skin is valuable,' he replied. 'I caught it yesterday and I'm only asking 40 yuan for it.'

'Do you realize that it is a protected species in China and you are likely to go to prison if we send for the police?'

We were neither of us sure if this was the case, but it worked and he hurriedly dropped the price to 10 yuan, which Louella handed him. I ran back to our bus and fetched the now empty sack in which the horses' corn had been kept. When I returned the man had lifted the badger off the ground by the wire so that it dangled by its hind leg. I made him put it down, at which the crowd leapt back in alarm, then taking the wire from him I managed to guide the badger into the sack without getting bitten. Keeping the wire out of the sack's mouth and supporting the animal's weight from below, I carried it back to the bus and told our rather surprised crew to drive out along the road to the north, towards the Wall and the desert. After a time we came to a wild spot where there was a grove of poplars at the junction of two streams and a patch of rough uncultivated scrub.

The release went unexpectedly easily. We laid Louella's thick saddle cloth over the sack to hold the badger down gently and eased its hind leg out. The wire only needed to be unwound and the skin below was unbroken. The pad of the foot was soft like a puppy's and the bone of its leg felt straight and undamaged. We opened the sack's mouth and the badger shuffled out. Its face and eyes were still dusty from the market and for a moment it paused, disorientated, to look up at us. Then it moved off in a hurry through some thick grass and into a gully.

What impressed me about all the Chinese who assisted in this little exercise was not that they let me do something which must have seemed pretty silly to them, but that they understood exactly why I was doing it. Although conservation is not practised yet to any great extent in China, thanks to television and a certain amount of propaganda it is beginning to be a recognizable concept. After all, the panda is the best known symbol of both China and the World Wildlife Fund – and badgers do look a bit like pandas. Perhaps this is one area where, along with the tree planting programme and the fight against the encroaching desert, there is hope for the future. In other areas I am less optimistic that improvements will come quickly.

Jonathan Fryer said of China in 1975 that it 'remains one of the least Westernized of all the countries of Asia'. I do not believe that a decade and more later that is still the case. Where all the efforts of the British, French, German, Japanese and Americans failed to colonize either the soil or the minds of the Chinese, the Cultural Revolution in particular and communism in general have to a large extent succeeded in destroying China's proud past. Chinese history, traditions and culture have been so undermined, rejected and scorned by the revolutionaries that everyone is now afraid of standing up for them. True, the surviving treasures of China's past have now been rehabilitated, if only because of the tremendous surge of tourism and the need to have guides and museums to cater for it. But the nature of art, even of skilful reproduction, is to be creative, and creativity has been beaten out of the Chinese over the last forty years. Those who were by birth, upbringing, education or inclination cultivated were pilloried, tortured or brainwashed until they recanted all such 'bourgeois revision-

206 馬 A Ride Along The Great Wall

ism', or they were killed. Anyone doubting this should read *Life and Death in Shanghai* by Nien Cheng, published shortly after our return from China, for a description of how it was only just possible for the very strongest of spirits to survive 'one of modern history's greatest aberrations'. Many of those who did survive then left the country if they could, as did Nien Cheng, after spending six-and-a-half years in solitary confinement subject to constant brutality and pressure to confess to crimes she had never committed. She writes:

... during the Cultural Revolution millions of men and women had been ordered to give up their jobs in the cities to settle in rural areas to receive re-education through physical labour. Those intellectuals allowed to remain in the cities were assigned the work of common labourers in their organizations. It was the practice of that time to have medical doctors emptying bedpans in the hospitals, professors cleaning toilets in the universities and artists and musicians building walls and repairing roads. While they were doing all these things, they had to attend struggle meetings and political indoctrination classes at which they had to abuse themselves by 'confessing' to their 'crimes'. Indeed, Mao's abuse of intellectuals reached an unprecedented level of cruelty during the Cultural Revolution. It very nearly destroyed China's tradition of respect for scholarship. During that time, anywhere in China, a man found reading a book other than Mao's four slim volumes ran the risk of being labelled as someone opposed to Mao.

Those who might have grown up respecting beauty and culture learned to despise it instead. Now, having seen so many changes of policy, when it comes to eulogizing and learning to appreciate China's past their hearts are not in it. As a result all that it is safe to respect is modernity at its most crass and utilitarian. Anything that smacks at all of style or quality, let alone the baroque or the eccentric — surely the very stuff of creativity — is feared.

Sadly, the soul of China felt dead to us and her beauty slept. But I cannot believe that the giant dormant legacy of 4,000 years of leading the world in taste and inventiveness can be subdued for ever. One day we will surely see a cultural renaissance in China, but it will be tinged with deep regret for all that has been destroyed.

The change will take time, for China is saddled with two obstacles to progress. One is a grinding bureaucracy which smothers initiative, creating delays and restrictions which stifle action. The other is the innate, but now largely groundless arrogance which prevents them listening to advice. Jonathan Fryer also speaks of an 'abstract Great Wall . . . a defence against the outer world behind which a satisfied population developed its philosophy'. We found that Wall, too, to be there still. But just as with the real Wall, the great Empire it once defended no longer exists.

Riding beside the Great Wall for 1,000 miles (1600 kilometres), we had a rare taste of China and that was all we sought. This was no epic journey proving man's mastery over actual obstacles or discovering unknown mysteries. We had a chance to see something of a maddening, confusing – yes, inscrutable – country from a perspective which no one else has been granted since Liberation. Mounted on our horses we had time to think and to observe the country with a much greater freedom than those hemmed in by the claustrophobia all tourists feel in China.

One day soon, I hope, the Chinese authorities will feel able to allow foreign travellers to see the whole of the Great Wall. Then perhaps someone will follow in William Geil's footsteps all the way from Shanhaiguan to Jiayuguan without a break. If they are lucky and have no problems they should be able to do it comfortably in the eighty days we originally allowed ourselves. If by then the security neurosis has calmed sufficiently to let them camp en route, they should have a wonderful time. The people they will meet along the way are among the kindest and the most hospitable to be found anywhere and the scenery, enhanced by the thread of Wall running through it, is unrivalled. Whoever they are and wherever they go, I beg them to do it on horses, good ones which they have chosen carefully. Then they will, I believe, experience China at its best and from the finest vantage point, as we did.

BIBLIOGRAPHY

BERTIN, M. *China: its Costume, Arts, Manufactures etc.* (Stockdale, 1813)

BONAVIA, DAVID. (intro.) *China Unknown* (Hodder & Stoughton, 1985)

BONAVIA, DAVID. *The Chinese* (Penguin, 1980)

BRIDGE, ANN. *The Ginger Griffin* (Chatto & Windus, 1934)

BRIDGE, ANN. *Peking Picnic* (Chatto & Windus, 1932)

BUTTERFIELD, FOX. *China, Alive in the Bitter Sea* (Hodder & Stoughton, 1982)

CABLE, MILDRED AND FRENCH, FRANCESCA. *The Gobi Desert* (Hodder & Stoughton, 1942)

NIEN CHENG. *Life and Death in Shanghai* (Grafton Books, 1986)

COTTRELL, STAN. *To Run and Not Be Weary* (Fleming H. Rivell, 1986)

CROW, CARL. *Handbook for China* (Kelly and Walsh, 1933/Oxford University Press, 1984)

CHENG DALIN. *The Great Wall of China* (South China Morning Post, 1984)

DE GOYER, PETER AND DE KEYZER, JACOB. *An Embassy from the East Indian Company of the United Provinces to the Grand Tartar Cham Emperor of China* (John Ogilvy, London, 1669)

DODWELL, CHRISTINA. *A Traveller in China* (Hodder & Stoughton, 1985)

FLEMING, PETER. *News from Tartary* (Jonathan Cape, 1936)

FLEMING, PETER. *One's Company* (Jonathan Cape, 1934)

GAUNT, MARY. *A Woman in China* (T. Werner Laurie, 1914)

GEIL, WILLIAM EDGAR. *The Great Wall of China* (John Murray, 1909)

GOULLART, PETER. *Princes of the Black Bone* (John Murray, 1959)

HOPKIRK, PETER. *Foreign Devils on the Silk Road* (John Murray, 1980)

HUNTINGTON, MADGE. *A Traveller's Guide to Chinese History* (Henry Holt, 1986)

KAPLAN, FREDERIC AND SOBIN, JULIAN. *Encyclopedia of China Today* (Macmillan, 1982)

KARLGREN, BERNHARD. *Sound and Symbol in Chinese* (Hong Kong University Press, 1971)

KIELD, DAVID. *All the Emperor's Horses* (John Murray, 1961)

LANGDON, WILLIAM. *China and the Chinese* (Chinese Collection, London, 1843)

MAILLART, ELLA. *Forbidden Journey* (William Heinemann, 1937/Century, 1983)

MEYER, CHARLES. *China Observed* (Hachette, 1981)

NEEDHAM, JOSEPH. *Science and Civilisation in China* (Cambridge University Press, 1971)

NEWBY, ERIC. *A Short Walk in the Hindu Kush* (Secker & Warburg, 1958)

NORMAN, HENRY. *The Peoples and Politics of The Far East* (T. Fisher Unwin, 1895)

RODZINSKI, WITOLD. *The Walled Kingdom* (Flamingo Fontana, 1984)

SAMAGALSKI, ALAN AND BUCKLEY, MICHAEL. *China A Travel Survival Kit* (Lonely Planet [Australia], 1984)

SAUNDERS, IRENE. *The Right Word in Chinese* (The Commercial Press [Hong Kong], 1986)

SERMEDO, FATHER ALCAREZ. *The History of that Great and Renowned Monarchy of China* (John Crook, London 1655)

SMITH, D. HOWARD. *Confucius and Confucianism* (Paladin, Granada, 1974)

SNOW, EDGAR. *Red Star over China* (Victor Gollancz, 1937)

SUMMERFIELD, JOHN. *Fodor's People's Republic of China* (Hodder & Stoughton, 1985)

HAN SUYIN. *A Many Splendoured Thing* (Panther, 1972)

TIME LIFE BOOKS. *China* (Time Life, 1984)

MAO TSE-TUNG. *Quotations from the Chairman* (Foreign Languages Press, Peking, 1967)

WARNER, LANGDON. *The Long Old Road in China* (Arrowsmith, 1927)

WARNER, MARINA. *The Dragon Empress* (Weidenfeld & Nicolson, 1972)

WAUGH, TERESA (trans.). *The Travels of Marco Polo* (Sidgwick & Jackson, 1984)

WICKERT, ERWIN. *The Middle Kingdom* (Harvill Press, 1983)

WYND, OSWALD. *The Ginger Tree* (Century, 1985)

ZEWEN, LUO. *The Great Wall* (Michael Joseph, 1982)

HAN ZHONGMIN AND DELAHAYE, RUPERT. *A Journey through Ancient China* (Muller, Blond and White, 1985)

CAO XUEQIN. *The Story of the Stone*. Also known as *The Dream of the Red Chamber* (Penguin, 1973)

INDEX

www.horsetravelbooks.com

HorseTravelBooks.com exists for two reasons - to encourage YOU to undertake a life-changing equestrian journey - and to keep us in the saddle.

The company was started by Basha and CuChullaine O'Reilly, as a natural outgrowth of The Long Riders' Guild, the world's first international organization of equestrian explorers and long distance travellers, which we helped to form.

The books we publish reflect what we ourselves passionately believe in – fewer physical possessions, individual freedom, the ancient bond between human and equine, and the mutual search with our horses for personal growth and boundless geographic horizons.

Having ridden in various countries and on four continents, CuChullaine and Basha can attest to the fact that before the formation of **horsetravelbooks.com** there was a global-wide lack of knowledge regarding equestrian travel. For 30,000 years brave men and women had been climbing onto horses and setting off in search of adventure and freedom. Yet despite being mankind's oldest link with the horse, this timeless equestrian legacy, and its attendant books full of accumulated knowledge, had nearly disappeared, not just from the marketplace, but from all human memory. So **horsetravelbooks.com** was created to put all the great equestrian travel tales into print, in their original languages, for the first time in human history.

With more than 60 of these titles currently for sale in three languages – including Aime Tschiffely's books – we are on our way to achieving this goal. Yet there are a minimum of 100 other known equestrian travel books still to be republished. We hope to have all of these amazing books available, in their 17 original languages, by the year 2005.

Plus, although we are currently about to release several of the most famous nineteenth century equestrian accounts ever written, we are very proud to announce that **horsetravelbooks.com** is now working with the legendary Long Rider, George Patterson, to republish his classic equestrian travel book "Journey With Loshay". This best-selling story describes George's equestrian adventures in 1940's Tibet, including his subsequent role in rescuing the Dalai Lama from the oncoming Chinese Communist Army. The original book will be augmented with never-before-seen material about George's later adventures with Tibetan rebels in the early 1950s.

In addition, we are putting the finishing touches on "The Long Riders", the world's first anthology of equestrian travel tales. Filled with the mounted adventures of daring men and women, "The Long Riders" is guaranteed to pin you in your seat, or drive you to the saddle.

And we are thrilled to report that Gordon Naysmith is now working with **horsetravelbooks.com** to publish his previously-unseen story. Tentatively entitled "A Will to Win", Gordon's book is delivered in diary form, and recounts his amazing 13,000 mile equestrian journey from South Africa to Austria in the early 1970s. It is an absolutely electrifying story of how he, and his unshod ponies, avoided horse-eating lions in Africa, nearly died of thirst in the deserts of Arabia, and finally came to grief in Western Europe.

Our list of titles is constantly changing, so please check our website, **www.horsetravelbooks.com**, for the latest information.

To learn more about past, current and future equestrian journeys, please visit The Long Riders' Guild website, the largest repository of equestrian travel in human history – **www.thelongridersguild.com**.